DEDICATION

For
David S.C. Kim
~wise father, dear friend~

CONTENTS

Introduction

Herbert Richardson

The essays in this volume were prepared in conjunction with conferences of the New Ecumenical Research Association (New ERA). This association promotes the development of theology which can unite Christian churches and other religions within the one family of God. Because this is the goal of the New ERA conferences, the essays were originally presented in a dialogue and discussion setting. They are intended to generate response from other theological and religious positions. Since this original setting cannot be included within this volume, the reader is urged to offer his own thoughtful response. Until a response is given, his reading will not be complete.

The New ERA purpose is similar to that of the Unification Church: to unify Christianity as a basis and example for establishing unity among the religions of the world. The image of this unity, we propose, is that of one family of religions. Within this family, the differences among religions are not destroyed. Rather, within this family, religions learn to respect and cooperate with one another in a natural way. Like Lessing, Sun Myung Moon considers Judaism, Christianity, and Islam to be brother and sister religions. Moon has also described the Unification Church as a "younger brother" to Christianity. The use of the word "brother" allows us to think of the Unification Church as different from other Christian churches, but still part of the same family.

The Unification Church, on this view of the matter, is our young Asian brother. Its leader, and many of his followers, have yellow skins.

Their religion presupposes Asian conceptions of reality, Asian family patterns, and Asian political concerns. Christian churches have learned how to accept the Germanic Christmas tree as not inconsistent with the Christchild; the question today is whether a Korean notion such as "God's Birthday" or the "arranged marriage" can also be recognized as legitimate cultural concomitants to true Christian faith.*

Generally speaking, all of the essayists in this volume approach the Unification Church in a friendly way. That is, they are willing to respect its own claims to be a "younger brother" to the Christian churches. But what that might mean for the Christian family—a new child arriving on the scene just as the older siblings (Protestant, Catholic and Orthodox) were learning to get along with each other—remains to be seen. It is one of the more ironic aspects of New ERA conferences that Catholic, Protestant and other theologians who previously would never have cooperated theologically now sit amicably side by side discussing the legitimacy of their young Moonie brothers. But it is not surprising that theologians who have been deeply affected by the recent Catholic-Protestant rapprochement would also be inclined to consider, patiently and charitably, Unification claims to be Christian, too.

In this volume, three of the essayists are Roman Catholic and one is a Jew (Clark, Flinn, McGowan and Rubenstein). The other essayists are Protestants from both sides of the schism: liberal and evangelical. They all are interested in the origins, implications and identity of the Unification Church. In some cases, they ask whether that new younger brother is truly legitimate; but in no case is there willingness to throw him out of the household. Rather, their goal is—respecting the Parenthood of God over all peoples, no matter how strange—to try to understand the new arrival.

Here he comes now—our new Unification brother—with Bible in hand and proclaiming a new interpretation: the "Divine Principle." Actually it was an Australian Pentecostalist who suggested to the first Korean followers of Moon that the best English translation for his

---

*In this volume the essays by Richard Rubenstein and T. James Kodera directly address the issue of Asian Christianity and the problems of cultural accommodation.

teaching should be "Divine." Moon's teaching is called in Korea, "the Principle," an expression which resonates with the ancient Confucian teaching that a just man is ruled by a right knowledge called the Yi (principle). There is no insinuation of "Divine-ness" implied in the Korean word; only the conviction that a human being must live according to what is best and highest if he is to be just.

Where does Moon find this "Principle" which guides human life toward maturity? In the Bible! Confucius proclaimed "the Principle," but Moon believes "the Principle" is embodied in the biblical story which finds its concrete perfection in Jesus Christ. This very Korean way of thinking about the Bible raises questions. If the Biblical revelation is thought of as the "Principle," if man is primarily a *family being*, if the power of the resurrection is the restoration of perfection to human life (all Asian presuppositions), then are we still dealing with "Christianity"? Tertullian asked "What has Athens to do with Jerusalem?" Today the question is "What has Jerusalem to do with Pyongyang?"

The strongest opponents of the Unification Church today are the continuing Tertullianists. Those who still oppose the ancient Hellenization of Christianity are, quite consistently, the most vocal opponents of its contemporary Asianization. Those who deny that Jesus is the *logos* also will deny that Jesus is the *yi*. Those Tertullianists believe that the uniqueness of Christianity is what sets it in stark contrast to other religions rather than what gives it the power to unite them all in itself.

Early theologians saw in Christianity not merely another religion, but another religion of another type. It was a "meta-religion," one which could include other religions in itself by raising them to a higher level. For example, Athanasius interpreted the Trinity as a way of affirming the truth of both Greek polytheism and Hebrew monotheism, while uniting both on a higher level. Standing in this same tradition, the Unification Church sees Christianity as a religion to unite all religions.* The very Asian elements in Unification evidence, its

---

*Lonnie Kliever, in this volume, also argues that the Unification Church takes a "Metainstitutional" form.

proponents argue, that it is a version of Christianity which is effectively accomplishing Christianity's highest task: restoring the unity of religions as the basis for restoring the unity of the human race.

For those who are already convinced "Hellenists," the Unification understanding is a happy development. To unite Pyongyang, the "Jerusalem of Asia," with the Jerusalem of the West is to initiate a great stage in Christian missions. But what does this undertaking mean for Christian theology? What does it mean for specific theological topics? Several of the essays in this volume address the doctrinal questions specifically (Sontag on God, Richardson on man, Clark on sin, Foster on Christ, McGowan on the Christian life). These essays are here published not as definitive statements but as opening gambits in a discussion on doctrinal development that, we are convinced, will continue for many decades. The discussion between Christianity and Asia, and between Asian Christianity and Western Christianity, has just begun.

Every western theologian who visits Asia is sure to be impressed by the lack of indigenous originality among Asian theologians. Students in Tokyo or Seoul or Taipei study Barth, Tillich, Temple, and Niebuhr. In fact, when the late Carl Michælson wrote his *Japanese Contributions to Modern Theology* he had to ignore (and thereby insult) the entire Japanese theological establishment. The theological establishment in Asia, noted Michælson, has made no original contribution to Christian theology. It has only reiterated what the original missionaries taught.

But as generations pass, reiterative mentality gives way to originative mentality. Can anyone be surprised that, in second and third generations, Asian Christians abandon Kantian and Aristotelian expressions of Christianity and begin to rethink the Bible in terms of their own philosophical and cultural traditions? Can anyone be surprised that this project is now most fully advanced in Korea—which is the only Asian country in which the nineteenth-century mission movement managed to succeed? Any visitor to Korea sees, in the churches, everywhere the evidence that this is a Christian country—the only Christian country in Asia (except for the Philippines). From this small

Asian Christian country comes the first Asian Christian church which establishes a strong missionary movement to the West! This is why, in my judgment, the Unification Church is so worthy of study—and is such an encouragement for Christian hope.

I myself, for these and many other reasons, have learned much from *Divine Principle*. My own essay in this volume expresses a clarified conception of sin and freedom which I have developed in close conversation with this text. I do not, however, wish to drape the other contributors in this volume with the same "Moonie Supporter" sash I myself parade. The other contributors, though all amiably and generously ecumenical, wear their own several sashes: "Moonie Admonisher," "Moonie Explainer," "Moonies—Separated Brother," "Moonie Psychoanalyzer," "Moonie Comparer," and "Ex Oriente Lux." The sole thing we several authors have in common is to have dined with Moonies, as their guests, and enjoyed the after-dinner conversation. What follows, in this volume, is a very small selection from among our memories of those happy times.

The preparation of a multi-author volume such as this always involves many more contributors than those whose names appear on the cover. There are several theologians whose essays, for reasons of space and time, must be postponed to a later volume. Copyediting and proofreading were done by Sylvia Grahn, Jack Kiburz, Jaime Sheeran, John Sonneborn, and Sarah Witt. Lynn Musgrave supervised production. I thank them all for their part in this production.

CONTRIBUTORS

Frederick Carney
Professor of Ethics, Perkins School of Theology, Southern Methodist University, Dallas, Texas

Francis Clark
Reader in Religious Studies, Open University, London; former Professor of Dogmatic Theology at Gregorian University, Rome

Frank K. Flinn
Consultant in Forensic Theology

Durwood Foster
Professor of Christian Theology, Pacific School of Religion and Graduate Theological Union, Berkeley, California

Lonnie D. Kliever
Professor and Chairman of Religious Studies, Dedman College of Southern Methodist University, Dallas, Texas

T. James Kodera
Chairman and Associate Professor of Religion, Wellesley College, Wellesley; Research Associate in East Asian Studies, Harvard University, Cambridge, Massachusetts

Thomas McGowan
Associate Professor of Religious Studies, Manhattan College, Bronx, New York

Herbert Richardson
Professor of Religious Studies, University of Toronto, Canada

Richard L. Rubenstein
Robert O. Lawton Distinguished Professor of Religion, Florida State University, Tallahassee, Florida

Frederick Sontag
Professor of Philosophy, Pomona College, Claremont, California

Letter to the Faculty, Perkins School of Theology

Frederick Carney

Within the last nine months my wife and I have attended two major conferences of the Unification movement as guests of that movement. The first was the Ninth International Conference on the Unity of the Sciences (ICUS) sponsored by the International Cultural Foundation and held November 26-29, 1980, (Thanksgiving weekend) at Miami Beach. The second was a Conference on Unification Theology sponsored by the New Ecumenical Research Association (New ERA) and held August 1-9, 1981, in the Canary Islands. It occurs to me that you might find my observations and reflections on these two conferences of some use to you in forming your own judgment concerning the Unification Church and the larger movement it has spawned. Therefore I take this opportunity to report to you.

The first conference (the Ninth ICUS) was less revealing of the thought and practice of the Unification movement than the second, so I shall comment quite briefly on the first and devote most of this communication to the second. The first was typical of the various ICUS's in that it was attended by several hundred scientists and humanists from many countries, that it addressed various issues about the relation of values to the sciences under this year's general rubric of "Absolute Values and the Search for the Peace of Mankind," and that its sponsor did not appear to inject any particular message or point of view into the conference (except, of course, for the sponsor's generally-announced interest in working toward the unification of the sciences and in relating values to them). Rev. Sun Myung Moon addressed an opening plenary session on the topic of the conference, arguing (not very well, I thought) from general philosophical grounds rather than from Unification theology as such. And at the closing banquet a Unification musical group performed. Otherwise one was not particularly aware of the sponsoring movement, and the addresses and discussions were conducted in a completely free and open spirit.

The sessions I personally attended were, for the most part, quite good, better than those of most professional meetings in which I have been involved. These included a philosophical address by a Vice-President and Dean of Graduate Studies at a major university in Texas on "Happiness and the Good Life," another by the holder of a Chair in Philosophy at a major university in Arizona on "Protecting a Way of Life," a session on "Military Technology and the Individual" at which a remarkably good address was delivered by a consultant in international relations, who was also the wife of a TV personality—who was a conference participant as well, and a truly exciting session on "Wealth and Society" that centered around contributions by the Director of Canada's nuclear energy program (from its inception) and by the former Director of the Oak Ridge National Laboratory, now the director of the Insititute for Energy Analysis.

Assuming that what I experienced at the Ninth ICUS at Miami Beach is generally representative of what may be experienced at any other ICUS, there seems to be nothing reprehensible about the internal operation of these conferences. Indeed, there is much about them that is highly commendable. However, a criticism sometimes made of them is that, even if they are commendable in themselves, they nevertheless bestow respectability on a movement whose character is such as not to deserve such respectability. Whether this is a valid criticism or not obviously depends on what the character of the overall Unification movement is. And for this we must look beyond the ICUS's. One important source of information is the Canary Island Conference on Unification Theology that my wife, who was independently invited as a full participant, and I attended. It had as its explicit purpose the examination of both the theology and the practices of the Unification Church. It is therefore to this second conference that I now turn.

Although I did not make a precise headcount of those attending the Canary Island Conference, my rough calculations indicate that the number was probably around one hundred and eighty. Of these, about forty (roughly 22%) were members of the Unification Church and approximately one hundred and forty (roughly 78%) were not. Among the "Moonie" contingent were Mose Durst (President of the Unification Church in America), Neil Salonen (former President of the Unification Church in America, and now President of the International Cultural Foundation—the ICUS sponsor), David Kim (President of the Unification Theological Seminary in Barrytown, New York), and John Maniatis (Executive Director of New ERA—the sponsor of this and other Unification theology conferences and seminars). Also representing the "Moonies," and constituting about half of their contingent, were twenty Ph.D. students from ten universities (Harvard 4, Yale 2, Columbia 2, Fordham 1, Drew 3, Catholic 1, Vanderbilt 3, Chicago 1, Claremont 2, and Cambridge, England 1). What about the much larger group of participants who were not members of the Unification Church? This group contained sizeable numbers of both Protestants and Catholics, a few Jews and Muslims, and some secularists. Most were academics, including a considerable number of persons of some distinction in their respective academic fields. Over half of the non-"Moonie" participants were from the United States and Canada, but Western Europe and Africa were also well represented. Blacks from both North America and Africa were present in somewhat surprising numbers, and some of them played quite significant roles in the conference.

One of the notable features of the conference was the openness and non-defensiveness of the Unification members about their doctrines and practices. Although they wanted very much to inform us about their faith, they were also quite desirous of hearing our criticisms and unfailingly courteous in responding to them. This commendable manner was evident in the very structuring of the conference. For example, most of its plenary sessions juxtaposed (a) one or two lectures on major Unification doctrines by Unification members with (b) the reading of two critical papers (prepared and distributed to all participants in advance of the conference) on these same doctrines by two non-Unification participants. The giving of these advocacy lectures and the reading of these critical papers would then ordinarily be followed by extensive discussion from the floor (which characteristically included remarks quite critical of the Unification lecture(s) and the doctrines propounded therein), to which periodically brief opportunities to respond were provided the lecturer(s), the two paper readers, and one additional Unification member. During the week-long conference, there were eleven such lectures and fourteen such critical papers on the lecture topics. The eleven lecture topics were on: Creation (2), Fall (1), Jesus and Christology (2), Providential History (2), Eschatology and Second Coming (2), Critique of Marxism (1), and Unification thought generally (1). The critical papers, as well as many of the critical comments from the floor, were made possible by the reading of *Divine Principle* and other Unification writings on doctrinal matters provided to all participants months prior to the conference.

I gathered the impression throughout these plenary sessions that the Unification movement refrained from using its power (the bankroller and organizer of the conference) for the pursuit of any short-range advantage to itself and its theological beliefs, even to the point that it leaned over backwards in accepting for itself a special vulnerability by making provision in the very structuring of the conference for extensive criticism of its doctrines (and acceptance of vulnerability must have involved a very considerable act of trust on the part of the Unification movement). Furthermore, this vulnerability and trust must have been present even in the early stages of the development of the conference, for responsibility for organizing and conducting this conference was apparently turned over to a group of three persons, two of whom, though consultants to the New ERA, are not members of the Unification Church. Darrol Bryant is a mainline Protestant academic from Waterloo, Canada; Richard Quebedeaux is an Evangelical author from Berkeley, California; and John Maniatis is the New ERA Director. The plenary sessions, which were presided over either by Bryant or Quebedeaux, were exemplary in providing bountiful access to the discussion from the floor and in the consistent fairness and good grace with which this was done.

Far from exemplary, however, were most of the doctrinal lectures by various Unification Church members. Quite frankly, six of the eleven lectures were, in my judgment, of such poor quality as to be below the minimum level of acceptability for an academic audience, which this audience predominantly was. By contrast, the quality of the critical papers delivered by non-Unification participants was, for the most part, far superior to the lectures by Unification Church members. So were most of the contributions from the floor. Unfortunately, therefore, it was often the critical papers and sometimes the contributions from the floor, rather than the lectures themselves, that enabled the discussion of Unification doctrines to become focused and meaningful. What specifically was wrong with most of the lectures? Generally speaking, they succumbed to one or more of the following faults: they lacked clarity in the discussion of major concepts, made inadequate connections in the development of lines of thought, were naive about what is involved in making various kinds of theological claims, misused historical evidence, or were poorly delivered.

Eight of the eleven lectures were given by young people (Ph.D. students or staff members) largely lacking at this stage in their lives in the academic skills, experience, and insight appropriate to this audience. (The other three lectures—among the better ones, I thought— were given by Mose Durst (2) and Neil Salonen (1), each of whom, though not a trained theologian, has had many years of experience with Unification thought and practice.) Obviously, the organizers of this conference were placing a great amount of confidence in some of the youth of this movement. For they were willing to give young Ph.D. students and staff members most of the responsibility for presenting and defending the major doctrines of the Unification Church before a large, highly-trained, and critical audience. I consider this confidence in Unification youth was considerably overdone. It resulted in treating the non-Unification majority of the conference with considerable (though, I am sure, unintended) discourtesy. And it did not serve the best interests of the Unification Church to have its central affirmations so poorly represented in the lectures. Even among their Ph.D. students who were present it would have been possible to make better choices of lecturers. I came to know two Ph.D. students at the conference who, in my judgment, could probably have done considerably better jobs of lecturing than some of those selected to do so.

The examination of Unification theology (and practices) was not, however, limited to these plenary sessions (with their Unification lectures, critical papers, and extensive floor discussion). Much of the business of the conference took place in scheduled discussion groups, in optional sessions on special topics, and in informal conversation during breaks and over meals. A word about the discussion groups may be in order. The entire conference was divided into discussion groups, each of which met on several occasions during the week. All such groups were introductory, except one advanced seminar for those who had previously attended a Unification conference. My own group was composed of seventeen persons, including two Unification Ph.D. students (one from Harvard and the other from Catholic University). Unfortunately it was seriously weakened as a vehicle for dialogue because of a language problem between Italian and English. Four of the five Italians in the group could not understand English well enough to grasp what was occurring in English, and all but one of the English-speaking participants could not understand Italian well enough to grasp what was occurring in Italian. And no translation services were provided. My wife's group did not have any problem of this nature, and she felt the discussion was excellent. I also heard very good reports about other groups.

Nevertheless there were still occasional good moments of dialogue in my discussion group. And I found the two Ph.D. students to be enormously interesting in the way they understood Unification theology (and practices), in the shaping it seemed to be giving to their lives, and in the dialectic between their own personal commitment and their openness to critical inquiry through which they quite helpfully contributed to the group discussion.

What about the theology itself of the Unification Church? I obviously cannot discuss this theology in detail here. But there are two comments of a general nature I wish to make. First, a hermeneutic comment. *Divine Principle* (the primary text of the Unification Church) seems to me to have much in common with seventeenth-century Reformed dogmatics. I am not speaking here about specific content, but rather the assumptions the author (presumably Rev. Moon) must be making about how his readers experience themselves and their worlds, and the consequent manner in which he sets forth his theological claims. In my judgment, he has never really encountered the eighteenth-century Enlightenment or the nineteenth-century Historicism, and thus has not yet struggled with plausible ways of making religious affirmations in the twentieth-century West. But considering Rev. Moon's background, this is not surprising. For his root religious experiences apparently occurred within the cultural context of a very conservative Korean Presbyterianism, a kind of Calvinism that, for the most part, bypassed both Enlightenment and Historicism. Nevertheless, it seems to me to be to Rev. Moon's credit that he has at least some recognition of this problem, and that at least some of the thirty-some Ph.D. students now being trained in the theological programs of major American universities understand that one of the long-term assignments from their Church is to contribute to the reformulation of the Unification message in such a manner as to maintain Rev. Moon's essential intentionality while availing themselves of the best of modern scholarship in so doing. But I need to be cautious in making this point. For I am not clear as to the extent that they actually have this assignment nor the extent to which they may in the future be at liberty in "faithfully revising" the founder's religious affirmations and/or his manners of expressing them. But that there is movement of some sort in this direction at the present time does seem clear to me. And this obviously involved placing a great deal of confidence in the young men and women the Unification Church in America has selected for doctoral studies. (This high expectation of their Ph.D. students may also have led the Unification Church to overestimate their present capacities and appropriateness of the very important conference lectures whose execution I criticized above.)

The second comment pertains to the relationship of Unification theology to Christian theology. Specifically, is the Unification Church a Christian Church? I think not. Furthermore I think clearly not. I grant that Unification theology employs much of the history and doctrine of the Christian Church. I further grant that some of its variations in interpreting this history and doctrine are neither greater than nor of a different order from the variations of some churches we generally consider to be within the Christian community. But the question is whether the Unification Church's relation to the overall Christian Church is to be conceived analogically on the model, for the example, of Lutheranism or of Islam. Both Lutheranism and Islam employ Christian materials quite heavily. But Lutheranism is and Islam is not part of the Christian Church, just as Hasidism is and Christianity is not part of Judaism, and the Sufis are and the Bahai are not part of Islam. The issue in each of these instances is whether the new movement affirms or denies the central constitutive affirmation (or affirmations) of the "mother community." The Unification Church's interpretation of Jesus as one in a series of Biblical persons God has sent to restore fallen human beings, as one who partially failed in this mission because of his premature death, and as one who shall be superseded in a Second Advent by another (Rev. Moon?) who will fulfill Jesus' mission— this interpretation, I say—is a denial of the central constitutive affirmation of the Christian Church, and thus moves the Unification Church outside and beyond the Christian Church in which it was nurtured. Christians should therefore regard "Moonies" not as fellow Christians, I think, but very much as we regard Jews and Muslims. We should value them as children of God sharing with us in the love of God, as fellow bearers of human rights whose welfare we are called upon to pray and work for, and as persons deserving our respect for their conscientious efforts to live according to Truth as they know it (even though we understand that Truth somewhat differently). Furthermore, I would hope that we would accept their invitations to enter into dialogue with them on theological and community matters (as we do Jews and Muslims), and join with them in welfare programs to feed the hungry and minister to the sick (in which they, like we, are already heavily involved through their World Relief Friendship Foundation).

Now I want to say something about two practice areas of the Unification Church: (a) family life and (b) fund raising. Prior to attending the Canary Island Conference my wife and I had read a number of criticisms of Unificationists that pertained to young "Moonies" being separated from their families and "programmed" to an alien way of life in which they were no longer free to make their own decisions. Therefore, we took considerable pains at the conference to inquire of young members of the Unification Church about their personal experience and insight regarding family matters, as well as their knowledge of the experiences of Unification friends and acquaintances. Our response was very affirmative to what we heard, and I have no reason to doubt the honesty of the several young "Moonies" with whom we talked. But rather than repeating the conversations to you I think it is better to quote at some length a person who has studied this matter extensively and has represented the gist of the problem far better than I can. This is Joseph Fichter, the Jesuit sociologist. The following quotations are taken from his essay "Marriage, Family and Sun Myung Moon" in America (October 27, 1979).

> One of the more inflammatory charges against the Unification community is that membership is disruptive of family life. The new convert leaves home and family, brothers and sisters, to dedicate himself entirely to the religious calling. Parents sometimes charge that their children have been "brainwashed." Similar charges have been made about Catholic religious orders that lured a daughter to the convent or a son to the seminary. God's call must be obeyed even if parents are in opposition. Some Catholic parents have forbidden their teen-age children to attend charismatic prayer meetings lest they be drawn too frequently out of the family circle. The fact is that the great majority of Moonies continue to maintain cordial relations with their parents and family.

The marriage chances for a Moonie are limited in one direction and expanded in another. The member is not permitted to marry outside the family, that is, the spouse must be a fellow member of the movement. This is the same strict rule that governs the marriage of Salvation Army officers and the mate selection of Israeli Jews. It was the same rule against mixed marriages which has gradually lost its effectiveness in the Catholic Church. Any member who wants to marry outside the Unification community has obviously misunderstood the central significance of sharing religious values in life-long fidelity.

On the other hand, there is a broadening of marriage opportunities in the Unification approval of "mixed" marriages across ethnic and racial lines. The conventional American pattern of marrying someone of your nationality, and especially of your own race, is widely disregarded in this movement. At the most recent engagement ceremony, about one-third of the couples were interracial. The large Oriental membership, especially of Japanese and Koreans, makes available to Caucasians a prospect of marriage partners that they would not ordinarily have. Sharing the same religious convictions and practices provides a value that transcends racial preferences.

The Unification Church does not allow teen-age marriages among its members and thus avoids what seems to be one of the main stumbling blocks to marriage stability. Members must wait until they are 25 years old to marry, and the preference is that they delay even longer. The stages of formation and growth precede the stage of perfection. It is clear that Moonies do not rush into marriage, but then there is no need to hurry. The female members do not have to be anxious and nervous if they are not engaged before they are 30. Their religious calling is marriage, and Mr. Moon will find a spouse for them and preserve them from living out their lives as old maids.

Marriage is a serious and holy sacrament for which lengthy preparation is required, and one of the notable aspects is the willingness of the members to have Mr. Moon pick their life partners for them. The concept of "arranged" marriages is alien to young Americans although it has been an accepted pattern for most of humanity during most of history. This is not a compulsory arrangement. Members are urged to express their preferences, but they do have a deep trust in Mr. Moon as the voice of God for them. One recently engaged man remarked:

"You try to have confidence in your prayer life that God knows what is best for you, that He will work through Reverend Moon to suggest the proper match for you."

According to the theology of *Divine Principle*, the revealed scripture of the Unification Church, God intended Adam and Eve to marry and have perfect children who would populate His physical kingdom. This intention was frustrated when Eve was sexually seduced by the archangel Lucifer, committing the original sin of adultery and causing the spiritual fall of mankind. Her impurity was passed on in premature and illicit intercourse with Adam, causing the physical fall of man. Later, God sent Jesus to redeem mankind from sin. He accomplished His spiritual mission, but He was killed before He could marry and father a new race of perfect children. Our first parents threw away God's love; Jesus was prevented from completing the redemptive mission on which His heavenly Father had sent Him.

The time has now come for the members of the Unification Church to establish perfect families in love and justice and unity, which in turn will unify all races, all nations, all religions. The divine scheme of love and family is laid out in the "four-position foundation," which appears to be cumbersome theological and relational formula. The four positions are: God, husband, wife and child. The pure and perfect relationship with God helps to establish the perfect relationship between husband and wife, and then between parents and children. The spiritual and physical kingdom of God, the total salvation that God intended in sending the Messiah, will be achieved by the ever expanding network of such God-centered families.

Conventional Christian theologians find these teachings rampant with heresy, but a pragmatic sociologist is likely to say that the Moonies have come upon a family program that works. While marriage counselors and parish priests are wringing their hands over the breakdown of family life, the Unification Church is doing something about it. The God-centered family is not merely a nice slogan or a spiritual ideal suggested by the church leaders. It is the essential core of community among the faithful of the church. It is also a deeply motivated system for restoring marital fidelity and family stability to modern society.

Whatever else one may say in criticism of the Unification Church as a social and religious movement, one has to recognize its systematic program for the restoration of "old-fashioned" morality, its emphasis on chastity before marriage, prayerful preparation for marriage, a readiness to accept guidance in the choice of a partner, marital love reflective of love of God, transmission of spiritual perfection to children. There has been much comment and criticism of the theological, political and economic aspects of the Unification Church, but very little has been said about the positive value implications in regard to marriage and family.

Obviously such a God-centered family practice requires an enormously high level of personal commitment. Furthermore, it contains some elements (e.g., arranged marriages) that are so different from contemporary fashion in the West as to be occasion for anxiety (even fear and animosity) on the part of some parents of newly-converted "Moonies." On the other hand, the Unification members with whom my wife and I talked at the Canary Island Conference seemed to us to be both free and happy in their commitment to this very demanding way of life, to its sexual, marital, and familial implications, and to the theological understanding upon which it rests. Nevertheless, two of them did observe that they felt the Unification Church in America had not earlier seen the importance of encouraging their new converts to be effectively related (at least so far as possible) to their parents, and that this was a mistake that, for the most part, has since been corrected. In any event, I find little, if anything, morally reprehensible in the Unification practice of sex and family life, and certainly nothing to justify the kidnapping and coercive deprogramming of new converts who are of age to make life decisions for themselves. To the contrary, I think their sex and family ethic is admirable (including its religious seriousness and racial inclusiveness), and I deplore the ominous violations of basic rights to which new converts have sometimes been put by bigoted deprogrammers and misguided parents.

Regarding this matter, I was pleasantly surprised to discover that a number of Black civil rights leaders were present at this conference (for example, Osborne Scott of New York, C.T. Vivian of Atlanta, and David Eaton of Washington, D.C.). They not only participated in the theology discussions, but also devoted a considerable amount of their "free time" to organizing political, religious, and media initiatives to combat flagrant misrepresentations of the Unification Church (and other new religious groups) by mass media and legislative interference with their religious and social liberties. The major coordinating vehicle employed in these efforts is the Committee Against Racial and Religious Intolerance, whose chairman is Dr. Osborne Scott. I was much encouraged to discover these Black civil rights leaders who had fought for the rights of their own people in the fifties and sixties now taking a leading role in support of the civil rights of other groups. As one of them told me, "The Unification Church is experiencing some of the same kind of media misrepresentation and oppressive legislation that we Blacks have long encountered."

Recently Governor Hugh Carey vetoed one such bill that passed the New York legislature. It would have provided for the involuntary removal from a group of a person who had undergone substantial behavioral change in response to "deceptive persuasion" by that group, and for the appointment of a temporary guardian over that person. More ominous, however, is an anti-"Moonie" bill Representative Ottinger of New York is circulating prior to introducing it in the U.S. House of Representatives. These Black leaders are working through the Committee Against Racial and Religious Intolerance and other organizations to oppose it. Regarding the Ottinger bill, the New York Civil Liberties Union states:

> This bill would create a federal felony punishable by up to five years imprisonment and a five thousand dollar fine. It would be violated by anyone who "with intent to persuade...any individual to become affiliated with...any organization, knowingly ...conceal(s) any material fact...in promoting affiliation by such individual with such organization and...attempt(s) to coercively prevent such individual from...contacting any individual not affiliated with such organization...by means of any communication in interstate commerce...." Other individuals and actions are swept into the bill also, but the extracted language is the core.
>
> The bill would criminalize evangelical and recruitment conduct not only by religious but by other membership organizations. Its thrust and structure are such that it is an invitation to

selective enforcement against unpopular and minority groups.

If the bill is designed to regulate criminally coercive conduct in interstate commerce, it is redundant. If it is designed to ensnare the unwary evangelist, it is unconstitutional. It would inevitably lead to entanglement with religious matters in attempting to isolate and define "material facts" about the theology and organization of churches and other groups.

It is a bill which can serve no legitimate purpose and is subject to substantial abuse.

I turn now, and much more briefly, to the other practice area of the Unification Church I mentioned earlier, fund raising. One of the decisive features of the Unification Church, I was told at the Canary Island Conference, is that all regular members have two continuing responsibilities: evangelism and fund raising. The fund raising takes many forms, ranging from soliciting contributions to participating in one of the Unification business enterprises (fishing and boat building were the two most frequently mentioned at the conference). The "Moonies" have received considerable criticism for deception in soliciting monies. I gather that at least some of this criticism was justified. I was told that there were times and places in the past that monies were solicited for one purpose and used for another. I was also told that the Unification Church in America now knows of these incidents, and is determined that they shall not be repeated. I personally have no empirical evidence either of earlier deceptions or of present forthrightness in solicitation. Nor do I have any reason to doubt the accuracy of what was told me.

The Unification business enterprises are a subject of considerable controversy in the communities in which they are conducted and in the mass media. They do, of course, constitute competition for companies that have been established for a longer period of time. The charge sometimes made is that the Unification movement engages in unfair competition. The Unification leadership denies that there is anything unfair in what they are doing, that they receive no special tax advantages on these enterprises, and that they pay competitive (if not superior) wages to non-"Moonie" employees. Here again, I have no empirical evidence to present, but simply pass on to you the gist of the statements made to us at the conference.

Those of you who wish to pursue further these and other matters pertaining to the Unification movement might want to read either or both of two books that seem to me to be quite insightful, competent, and fair-minded. The first is a Sage Library of Social Research publication by two social scientists: David G. Bromley and Anson D. Shupe, Jr., *"Moonies" in America: Cult, Church, and Crusade* (Beverly Hills and London: Sage Publications, 1979), 256 pp. (Bromley and Shupe also have a later Sage book entitled *The Vigilantes: Deprogrammers, Anti-Cultists, and the New Religions.*) The second book is by a well-known philosopher-theologian: Frederick Sontag, *Sun Myung Moon and the Unification Church* (Nashville: Abingdon, 1977).

In conclusion, I want to say that I am very pleased to have been able to experience the Unification movement at first-hand through these two conferences in Miami Beach and the Canary Islands. I feel something like being "present at the creation" (to borrow a book title from Dean Acheson) of an exciting new religious movement. And I came away from these conferences with a very real respect for the Unification movement, and a willingness to join in cooperative endeavors with this movement in the future. But I am in no sense tempted to join the Unification Church. I think the Christian faith as presented by such interpreters as St. Paul, Augustine, Thomas Aquinas, John Calvin, and Reinhold Niebuhr presents a far more profound understanding of human existence than does Unification theology.

Horace Bushnell and the Unification Movement: A Comparison of Theologies

Thomas McGowan

One task of an emerging theology like that of the Unification Church is to appreciate the theological heritage which it shares with others and to avoid the arrogance of claiming that its ideas have somehow come forth full blown and absolutely novel. What I intend to do in this paper is to point out that some of the principal beliefs of Unification theology are at least quite compatible with the theology set forth in the nineteenth century by Horace Bushnell. It is not my purpose to show any direct or indirect link between Bushnell and Sun Myung Moon, but only to note the resonance of certain ideas. Of course, there are also many dissimilarities between Bushnell and Unification theology, but each gives explanations of certain key doctrines which are remarkably congenial to one another. I will illustrate this in six areas: original sin and its effects, the salvific role of Jesus, the place of sacrifice in redemption, the power of religious nurture, the tension between grace and freedom, and the shape of the future church.

1. Original Sin and Its Effects

Unification thought interprets the Genesis story of the Fall in terms of acts of illicit love, first between the serpent-Satan-Lucifer figure and Eve and later between Eve and Adam. For Adam and Eve it was not the sex act itself which was sinful, but rather the premature use of the act. Although God had intended to establish a perfect relationship with a mature Adam and Eve and to bless them with children in a sinless world, the sins of Satan and the primal parents disordered this ideal society. What Unificationists call a "blood relationship" with Satan was established and is passed down through the generations. What should have become a human family centered on God was frustrated and became one centered on Satan. Instead of the "Three Blessings" promised by God—individual perfection in personal maturity, social perfection in the family, and ecological perfection in dominion over the cosmos—mankind inherited the evil tendencies of Satan.

Like the Unificationists, Bushnell saw immaturity as the primary cause of sin. A person is born, he said, into a "condition privative," which is a moral state "inchoate or incomplete, lacking something not yet reached, which is necessary to the probable rejection of evil."[1] It is not ignorance of the law that leads to sin, he explained, but rather the need to verify the meaning of right and wrong through experience, much the same way as a child will touch fire because the knowledge of its ill effects has not yet been drilled into him by the process of experience.

Bushnell claimed that Adam, representing all mankind, manifested such a "condition privative" because he, as a man who had "just begun to be"[2] was not able to understand all the consequences of choosing evil nor had he sufficient practice in obeying the law. In addition, and this is very similar to the interpretation given by Unification theology, Bushnell related Adam's sin to his inexperience in dealing with what he called "malign powers."[3] Since a "just begun to be" Adam had no experience in recognizing and resisting the demonic forces, Bushnell concluded that he would be vulnerable at first to the temptations presented to him. Not that this lack of experiential knowledge took away guilt, Bushnell hastened to add, since a notional or theoretical knowledge of the law is sufficient to place us under obligation to it.

Sin for Bushnell introduced discord into what would otherwise be the harmony of nature. The true story of sin, he said, is that "man turns God's world into a hell of misdirection."[4] This profound reality of disorder produces ill effects in the individual, in society, and in the physical world, much in the same way as sin negated the "Three Blessings" in Unification theology.

The individual is affected because sin causes a "breach of his internal harmony,"[5] which leads his will, judgment, and even his body into revolt, one against the other. Society is also affected because humanity is an organic whole, Bushnell asserted, and once disorder has been introduced into its very nature, it cannot propagate itself in any way that is unmarred. He explained that under the "physiological terms of propagation, society falls or goes down as a unit, and evil becomes in a sense organic in the earth."[6] Since there are moral connections between all people, it follows that the effects of sin are not shut up within the individual but are passed down through the human race. "If we are units," Bushnell wrote, "so also are we a race, and the race is one—one family, an organic whole; such that the fall of the head involves the fall of all the members."[7] When Adam sinned he originated evil effects which have disordered all succeeding generations. Under this doctrine of the headship of Adam, Bushnell saw expressed the social interaction of man's existence and the propagation of sin as family follows family. Once the society of families was infected with sin, it moved inexorably ahead, propagating evil as it propagated itself. Finally, the physical world, the third area affected by sin becomes in Bushnell's words a "realm of deformity and abortion," a universe "groaning with the discords of sin and keeping company with it in the guilty pains of its apostasy."[8]

2. Jesus Christ

In Unification theology the perfected Adam or the Christ is the one who has attained the full purpose of creation and assumes therefore " the divine value of God," has "an existence unique in the whole universe, " and indeed is "the substantial encapsulation of the entire cosmos."[9] To a degree Unification theology allows Jesus to be called this perfected man but it warns against identifying him with God.[10] The main role for Jesus seems to be that of messiah, whom Unificationists define as the one who is to bring about the ideal family and the Kingdom of God. Jesus, however, was not able to accomplish this physical regeneration of the human race and provided only a "spiritual salvation" through his crucifixion and resurrection. Since

Jesus and the Holy Spirit accomplished only the mission of spiritual "true parents," it is the Unification expectation that another messiah is needed to form the human family in a proper relationship with God.[11]

Although Bushnell would most likely have had great difficulty with the interpretation of the messianic office as one of marriage and parenting, he would have been quite sympathetic with the Unification hope of a human society in friendship with God. Like the Unificationists, Bushnell saw the essence of sin in alienation from God. He maintained that human therapy could not approach the core of the problem of sin, even though it might mitigate the most flagrant manifestations of injustice. Since a sinful human race is incapable of entering upon a proper relationship with God, what is needed is the discovery of God's presence in the world and his openness to holy community with mankind. Bushnell saw this revelation in Jesus Christ, who manifested God to mankind and offers again the reality of union with the divine.

Bushnell's was a high christology, summarized in his emphatic claim that "the pre-incarnate Son of the Father is the incarnate Son of Man."[12] For him Jesus Christ broke the organic force of evil by entering the world and "bringing into human history and incorporating in it as such, that which is Divine."[13] The incarnation raised humanity in this life to a new position which it could not have attained without the coming of the eternal God-man. The incarnation was not an adjustment in the plan of God, but the fulfillment of creation by the revelation of God's presence in the world as the source of holiness. Bushnell interpreted the atonement, therefore, in terms not of payment for guilt but of mankind's being "formed to Christ" and "divinized" by meeting God in Christ. It was the restoration of that community with God which mankind had originally enjoyed but which had been lost by sin. In order for humanity to be able to respond to God's invitation to fellowship, it was first necessary, Bushnell argued, that mankind be raised to the divine because "it is only in the pure divine that God can have complacence and hold communion."[14] Unlike Unification theology, therefore, Bushnell saw more at stake than a reorientation of the human community through new "true parents." For him it was essential that mankind be offered the chance of divinization and consequently of true community with God through the revelation of the incarnate Son of God.

3. Indemnity and Sacrifice

When Unification theology interprets the function of suffering in his work of the restoration, it starts by rejecting the idea that Jesus' death on the cross was part of God's original plan of salvation. The mission of Jesus was not to suffer and die but to reestablish the ideal family. When Jesus had been abandoned, Unificationists say, "God had to pay the price for the sinful lack of faith of the Israelites and all mankind by giving the life of his only son to Satan as a ransom." Jesus' death became the price for the redemption of mankind, but it was in his resurrection that "God opened up a way of spiritual salvation." Although the "physical selves of mankind are still subject to satanic invasion," their "spirit" can attain salvation.[15] The Unification theory is that although Jesus intended the complete salvation of mankind, he was frustrated and succeeded by his death and resurrection in saving mankind only in the spirit world. One noteworthy aspect of the doctrine is that it starts with a passable God who endures the death of Jesus.

"Indemnity" is the category under which Unification theology most systematically considers the place of sacrifice in the plan of restoration. Indemnity means that certain conditions must be met in order for something or someone to be restored to a position which has been lost. So it is that the human race, which has broken its original relationship to God, must restore the foundations on which to build a new relationship. What Unificationists call an "indemnity condition" achieves the restoration of a lost state by reversing the process which led to the loss in the first place. Sometimes the indemnity which is paid is equal to the loss ("eye for an eye"), sometimes it is less (faith yields abundant results), and sometimes it is more (the Israelites' wandering in the desert was extended from forty days to forty years because of their infidelity).[16] The whole human race must perform certain "indemnity conditions" before the messiah can be received and the Kingdom established. So also must individual Unificationists do "indemnity conditions" in order to restore proper human and divine relationships. These conditions include periods of prayer, fasting, and sacrifice.

Sacrifice also played a central role in Bushnell's theology, and like the Unificationists he too rejected the view that "the bleeding," as he called it, was the end of the incarnation instead of the reestablishment of community between God and mankind. For Bushnell, sin was humanity's failure to maintain friendship with God. The crucifixion, then, was not the object of Jesus' ministry, but the "bad fortune" his reconciling work was bound to encounter.[17] The true purpose of Jesus' death was to sensitize mankind to its isolation and to bring it again into friendship with God.

Bushnell rejected the unsophisticated idea of a direct substitution of pain for pain in such a way that "God accepts one evil in place of the other, and being satisfied in this manner, is able to justify or pardon."[18] Besides being basically unfair, he claimed, this teaching left no room for God's necessary participation in suffering. As he wrote, "The frown, then if it be said to be of God, is quite as truly on God. The expression of justice or abhorrence is made by sufferings that are endured, not out of the circle of divine government, but in it."[19] God suffers in order to make evil "what it is not; to recover and heal it."[20] Sacrifice, or what the Unificationists might call indemnity, is the offering of "one's ease and even one's personal comfort and pleasure to the endurance of wickedness, in order to . . . subdue it."[21] The return to the true relationship which existed prior to sin demands this kind of personal participation in suffering in order to break the spirit of alienation or sin in the world. If God were simply to "forgive and forget," there could be no true friendship because there could be no true basis of relationship. For God to be free for friendship with sinful humanity, explained Bushnell, he had to identify with sinners through suffering. The recovery of friendship is worked out "by the transforming powers of sacrifice," he wrote in words which Unificationists might not be surprised to find in Divine Principle, and "the whole plan centers in this one principle, that the suffering side of character has a power of its own, superior, in some respects, to the most active endeavors."[22]

Before true forgiveness of sins and reconciliation can happen, a change must take place in God as the wronged party. All love, whether in God or in mankind, is bound up with suffering, claimed Bushnell, and he saw Christ's vicarious sacrifice as a revelation of God's loving and therefore suffering nature. In imagery similar to the Unificationists' metaphor of God's "heart," Bushnell called this "a revelation in time of just that love that had been struggling always in God's bosom; watching wearily for the world and with inward groanings unheard by mortal ears."[23]

Bushnell comes closest to the Unification idea of indemnity when he analyzed the doctrine of forgiveness of sins not in terms of forgetting sin or of substituting for the sinner, but rather of breaking the hold of sin in history and returning creation to an originally pristine condition. What sin had done in history had to be undone. Christ had come, Bushnell said, not to obtain forgiveness of sin, but rather "to make sin itself let go of the sinner, and so deliver him inwardly that he shall be clear of it." The achievement of this goal requires, he explained, "an almost recomposition of the man; the removal of all his breakage, and disorder, and derangement, and the crystallization over again of all his shattered affinities, in God's own harmony and law."[24] Both Unificationists and Bushnell agree that this breaking down of sin and rebuilding of true humanity takes place cumulatively in history, growing and working over the centuries towards ultimate perfection. Unificationists have a predilection for charting history in elaborate schema of providential ages, and they see the final stages of restoration as now upon us in terms of a second advent of the messiah. Bushnell would not have accepted the need for a messiah after Jesus, but his ideas about the sanctifying effects of the power of Christ when it penetrates all aspects of society and the world could be preached comfortably by any Unificationist. As he described this power, "It penetrates more and more visibly our sentiments, opinions, law, sciences, inventions, modes of commerce, advancing, as it were, by the slow measured step of centuries, to a complete dominion over the race."[25]

4. Religious Nurture in the Family

Clearly, there is in Unification theology a doctrine of development. As *Divine Principle* says, "…everything made in the beginning was meant to be perfected through a certain period of time."[26] In order for a creature to be completed, it must advance in orderly fashion through the three stages of formation, growth, and perfection. The symbol in Unification thought for the desired goal of this process is the "four position foundation," in which God is the ultimate unifying center for all of creation. In terms of men and women, therefore, the whole point of the fall is simply that the human race has failed to go through the three stages and to establish a truly God centered set of relationships. Adam and Eve sinned by assuming the rights of perfected creatures while still in an immature stage of development. If, however, a mature Adam and Eve had become husband and wife, had children, and centered their society on God, then the whole universe would have become what *Divine Principle* calls a "spherical movement of unified purpose."[27] The stage of formation would have been achieved in individual maturation, growth in the establishment of the family, and perfection in the act of taking dominion over all things.

The Unification belief is that this process has broken down precisely at the point of the development of the family. Instead of blessed families populating God's kingdom with sinless children, the fallen world can only achieve defective families producing sinful generations. The restoration of the ideal family is at the heart of the Unification movement, therefore, and it is the reason why Unificationists believe in the need for a second coming of the messiah. In Unification thought Jesus intended to be the completed Adam by marrying, forming the ideal family, and beginning the true generation of God's people. Since Jesus was not able to accomplish this, it is the Unification belief that a second coming of the messiah is necessary so that the total salvation intended by God will be achieved in an ever expanding network of God centered families.

Bushnell also saw salvation in terms of nurture and especially nurture within the family. He reacted against the emphasis on individualism which lost sight of humanity's relational character, and he concentrated instead on the need for social experience of Christ. Revivalism was the usual answer to the question of salvation in the New England churches of Bushnell's time. This method of salvation stressed sudden commitment to the gospel, rather than the route of nurture. At the heart of revivalism was the belief that natural men and women could not grow in grace without first being reborn. This rebirth was seen as a vivid but private experience in which the individual turned to God. Conversion was overwhelming, transforming, ecstatic, but most of all, it was without mediation—no family, congregation, minister, or ritual stood between the convert and God. For the revivalist, people are not physically born into the church nor do they grow in piety, but they enter through a direct act of God.

Bushnell disagreed with the revivalist theology, especially over the issue of children, since it seemed to stipulate that children should grow up in sin so that they could eventually, in one dramatic experience of conversion, choose Christ and be saved. Nurture had taken a morbid and dangerous turn, he said, when children were taught to regard themselves as sinners rather than as Christians. A scheme based entirely on conversion "gives a most ungenial and forlorn aspect to the family," he noted, and "it makes the church a mere gathering in of adult atoms, to be increased only by the gathering in of other and more numerous adult atoms."[28] Such an individualistic approach to religion was at odds with Bushnell's social view of the Christian life. Since the spiritual life was for him a process of growth in friendship with God, he had to look for an economy of salvation which spoke to the issue of social nurture instead of private conversion.

One vehicle which Bushnell placed at the center of this nurturing process is the family. For him the family is not an aggregate of individuals but the primary social unit whose members are so deeply involved in mutual actions and attitudes that the child is inevitably formed by its power over character. The family is indeed like an organism, Bushnell claimed, because of the powerful psychological and physical bonds among the members. The effect of these forces is organic, since the family members are so locked together that they "take a common character, accept the same delusions, practice the same sins, and ought, I believe, to be sanctified by a common grace."[29] A Christian family can therefore configure the child to Christ even before the child could possibly choose Christ for himself or herself.

Like most contemporary developmental psychologists, Bushnell identified stages of growth in childhood. He saw two such stages, "the age of impressions" and "the age of tuitional influences, " or, as he also named them, "the age of existence in the will of the parent" and "the age of will and personal choice in the child."[30] He believed that in the first stage, the pre-language years, "more is done to effect, or fix, the moral and religious character of children…than in all the instruction and discipline of their minority afterward."[31] Language itself has no meaning until the seminal impressions coming from the life of experience give it an interpretation. Therefore, the child must first have some kind of experience of God before he or she can give any meaning to the word "God." Since the meaning of language must originate in impression derived from experience, Bushnell concluded that it is an error for theology to hold that nothing religious can be done for a child until the child is old enough to be taught by means of language.

Bushnell saw the family as a divinely constituted organ of regenerative grace. He defended his position not only with the psychological argument that the family is the social group in which the character of the child is formed, but also with the theological one that it is the sacrament of God's grace. He thought it incongruous to suppose that a child is to grow up in sin in order to be converted when he or she comes to the age of maturity. He proposed, on the contrary, "that the child is to grow up a Christian, and never know himself as being otherwise." In this way the child is "to open on the world as one that is spiritually renewed, not remembering the time when he went through a technical experience, but seeming rather to have loved what is good from his earliest years."[32] This makes sense, he said, because the times of infancy and childhood are most pliant to good. "How easy it is then, as compared with the stubbornness of adult years, to make all wrong seem odious, all good lovely and desirable."[33]

In language similar to that used in Unification theology, Bushnell explored the dynamics of both original sin and Christian nurture. He argued that close examination of the relation between parent and child would reveal laws of organic connection which make it natural to expect that the goodness or depravity of the parent would be propagated in the child. If, on the one hand, sin can be inherited, so also can virtue; one is as much a social product as the other. He wrote that the child is not "set forth as an overgrown man, issued from the Creator's hand to make the tremendous choice, undirected by experience," but is rather "gently inducted, as it were, by choices of parents before his own, into the habit and accepted practice of all holy obedience; growing up in the nurture of their grace, as truly as of their natural affection." And coming very close to the Unification doctrine of blessed children, Bushnell concluded that "as corruption or depravation is propagated under well known laws of physiology, what are we to think but that a regenerate life may be also propagated, and that so the Scripture truth of a sanctification from the womb may some time cease to be a thing remarkable and become a commonly expected fact?"[34] God's plan, as interpreted by him, was " to let one generation extend itself into and over another, in the order of grace, just as it does in the order of nature."[35]

It is most important to realize, Bushnell urged, that the forces at work in the family can be organized for good instead of evil. The Christian economy of salvation should aim to take possession of the organic laws of the family and use them as instruments of regeneration. These laws were intended for the nurture of virtue in the plan of God before the Fall, he argued, so it is only right that Christ reclaim and sanctify them for his own purposes. Again anticipating Unificationist ideas, Bushnell wrote that the family which has been seen only as "an instrument of corruption," is "to be occupied and sanctified by Christ, and become an instrument also of mercy and life." From this it will follow, he continued, "that the seal of faith, applied to households, is to be no absurdity; for it is the privilege and duty of every Christian parent that his children shall come forth into responsible action, as a regenerated stock."[36] So great was Bushnell's optimism concerning this work of regenerating the human "stock" that he envisioned a future similar to Unificationist expectations in which "grand consolidations and massings of society will be gathering heavier momentum and a more and more beneficent sway over the conduct and life of individuals." In this future world the Christian family will be the germ of a renewed race. "Good men will be born by nations," he prophesied, "—a nation is a day."[37]

5. Grace, Law, and "The Principle"

Unification theology sets the stage for its interpretation of the relation between God's will and mankind's freedom when it distinguishes between "indirect" and "direct" dominion. "Indirect" means the way God rules people while they are in an immature state. At this time God can govern only through the mediation of "The Principle." But even the autonomous action of "The Principle" is not enough, since people can realize their perfection only when they fulfill their personal responsibility to observe God's commandments. In the Unification understanding, God's rule is much vaster than mankind's, but the human decision-making factor is a necessary part of the maturation process. "Direct" dominion, on the other hand, means the way God will relate to perfected people in an unmediated fashion by love, or, in a favorite Unification metaphor, the way human beings will become one in "heart" with God.[38]

Unification thought struggles with the tension between "The Principle" and responsibility, much the same way as orthodox Christian theology struggles with grace and freedom. While on the one hand it sees "The Principle" as God's gift which saves, on the other it tries to preserve at least a small area for human input. Responsibility is an essential characteristic of human nature for Unificationists because it is in free action that humanity participates in creation and comes to assume, like God, a role of direct dominion over the rest of creation. Freedom, says *Divine Principle*, can exist apart neither from "The Principle," nor from the possibility of some meaningful human role in accomplishing God's purpose of creation.[39]

Bushnell likewise wanted to balance somehow the action of divine grace and human responsibility so that the converting power of

God would be preserved alongside the laws of natural development. In language similar to the Unificationists' "direct, indirect" phraseology, he claimed that there is at work a "fixed relation between God's mediate and immediate agency in souls," which values both God's grace and a person's receptivity.[40] A person is not completely passive in the work of salvation but must cooperate by being open to the gift of God's life. Although right intent by itself does not save, it is the necessary condition for the power of Christ to be effective.

According to Bushnell, God acts on the receptive person in a two-step program. First of all, he develops in the man or woman a true understanding of law out of the abstract and vague moral principles which are innate in the whole human race. Bushnell felt that it was important to place law properly in the system of God to show that "His world-plan, though comprehending the supernatural, will be an exact and perfect system of order, centered in the eternal unity of reason about His last end."[41] He warned that once religion is placed beyond the realm of law, it has already deteriorated into superstition. "Nothing is more certain or clear," he claimed, "than that human souls are made for law, and so for the abode of God." Without law, he said, souls "must freeze and die."[42]

The second step by which God acts on a person, according to Bushnell, is the gospel, which for him meant the person of Jesus Christ. The function of the law is to give knowledge of sin as an initial stage in the process of training in virtue, but it is in the meeting of Christ that lives are radically changed. Regeneration, he wrote, consists in "being trusting itself to being, and so becoming other and different, by a relation wholly transactional."[43] This completion of a person in the transforming relationship with God in Christ is what constituted salvation for Bushnell; it is not a transitory experience but an enduring friendship.

Like Bushnell, Unification theology has a two-step process leading to perfection. The first depends on "The Principle" to mediate God's dominion over creation, and the second involves direct union with God. Where Bushnell wrote "law," Unificationists with little difficulty can read "The Principle," which to them is "the basic active universal

law that originates in God and pervades the Creation."[44] Unificationists
believe that "The Principle," like Bushnell's "law," explains the inner
dynamics of God's creation, and so its practice is the way men and
women can mature. But as Bushnell looked beyond the "law" to the
"gospel," so also does Unification theology look beyond "The Principle"
to the "heart" of God. For both Bushnell and Unificationists this
second step is a mystical, transforming experience. It makes a person
"one in Heart with God," says Unification theology, and allows God to
rule directly by love.[45]

6. The Shape of the Future Church

Unificationists, almost by definition, look forward to the
restoration of what they consider to be God's original plan for the
unity of all aspects of human life. Since sin has fragmented creation,
the new age they hope for will be marked by the integration of what
now appear to be discrete entities. In order to help bring about this
new age, Unificationists engage in interracial marriages, work for the
unity of the sciences and of science and religion, and promote
ecumenical dialogues among members of different religions. The
ultimate goal of this unification process is a one-family world society.
When Unificationists speak of the future church, therefore, they
really mean a network of ideal families and not a special society of
people who have been "called out" from the family. In a sense the
"church" will disappear into the world family. For this reason many
Unificationists prefer to say they belong to a "movement" rather than
to a "church."

Bushnell also developed the ideal of an ecumenical church which
would eventually embrace the world, assimilating the insights of all
the varied sects in a comprehensive truth. But first of all, he said,
language must be seen for what it truly is, not the literal truth but
only the representation of truth. He claimed that there were two ages
in the history of the church—a first which sought literal truth in the
religious symbols and a second which was comprehensive. In the first
age people believed that it was possible to achieve a language which
could express exhaustively and for all time an unchanging content of

reality. They regarded the forms of truth as identical with truth itself and so had no choice "but to live and die by it, and no thought, perhaps, but to make others live and die by it too." Bushnell said this led not only to the controversies of the ancient church but even to those of his own century. In the second age, however, people will consider the beliefs of others and seek the partial truth in each symbol. "Under contrary forms are found common truths, and one form is seen to be the complement of another—all forms, we may almost say, the complement of all others."[46] Like the Unificationists, he suggested that such an age was, in fact, approaching:

> Accordingly, the eyes of men are now being turned, as never before, towards the hope of some new catholic age, where spirit and faith, having gotten their proper realm, clear of adverse possession, shall be able to abide there in God's simple light, to range it in liberty, and fill it with love.[47]

Bushnell argued that since the human mind is finite it can approach only a small part of the truth at once, or, as he put it, only the "hem of the garment." Each person in ignorance calls the hem the whole garment. It follows that people have created religious sects because of the peculiar grasp of the truth which each one possessed. But a more comprehensive method gives the hope of a wider view of truth by combining the opinions of all people. So it may come about that "after long ages of debate, wherein every part of the hem is brought into view," it will be possible "for any disciple, who will look through the eyes of all, to form to himself some view of it that is broader and more comprehensive."[48]

Such a comprehending of all truths reflected in the creeds of history presented for Bushnell the possibility of a new kind of ecumenical church in the future. And if such a church is ever to appear, he argued, where better than in the United States? God has called "all these diverse multitudes, Protestant and Catholic, together, in crossings so various, and a ferment of experience so manifold, that he may wear us into some other and higher and more complete unity than we are able, of ourselves, and by our own wisdom, to settle." The result of all this will be nothing less than "a perfected and comprehensive Christianity," he hoped, which will be "set up here for a sign to all nations."[49]

Bushnell saw the key to this new society in the separation of church and state decreed by the United States Constitution. Because of this, he said, "superstition is eaten away by the strong acid of liberty, and spiritual despotism flies affrighted from the broken loyalty of the metropolis."[50] Although one of the first results of this separation was, in fact, the development of sectarianism, he hoped for the eventual fruition of a radically new union of all religions in Christ. In his vision of this new order, people will look for good in each other rather than in orthodoxy. Likewise, the exchange of opinions "by travel and books, and the intermixture of races and religions" will result in broader views of Christian truth.[51] As an effect of these influences, he argued, church and state, which had to be parted in the process of developing freedom, would coalesce again once freedom has been attained, not as church and state any longer, but "in such kind of unity as well nigh removes the distinction—the peace and world-wide brotherhood, established under moral ideas, and the eternal truths of God's eternal kingdom."[52]

Like Unificationists, Bushnell anticipated the emergence of the universal church through the dynamics of the family. The church, he said, is not a collection of individuals but a new organism composed of Christian families. It acts to repair the disorder which sin has inflicted on creation and which the laws of nature would otherwise perpetuate. "Its very distinction as a redemptive agency," he wrote, "lies in the fact that it enters into nature, in this regenerative and rigidly supernatural way, to reverse and restore the elapsed condition of sinners."[53] The church is not simply a natural society, Bushnell insisted, but is indeed the Holy Spirit, who:

> ...collects families into a common organism, and then, by sanctifying the laws of organic unity in families, extends its quickening power to the generation following, so as to include the future, in all ages, becomes a body under Christ the head, as

the race is a body under Adam the head—a living body, quickened by him who has life in himself, fitly joined together and compacted by that which every joint supplieth.[54]

Bushnell held that such a shift from Adamic to Christed humanity is possible only by the power of God "to prepare the godly seed" and to establish Christianity as "the great populating motherhood of the world."[55] His expectation was that a "truly sanctified stock" would ultimately fill the earth. "Not that the bad heritage of depravity will cease," he wrote, "but that the second Adam will get into power with the first, and be entered seminally into the same great process of propagated life."[56] This future church will be marked by the disappearance of creeds and catechisms since the people will live in the truth. It will also have solved the apparent antagonism between science and religion, one of the goals of Unificationists. In this future church, "learning and religion, the scholar and the Christian, will not be divided as they have been."[57] He foresaw that the church will eventually attain what the prophets had predicted, namely, "a city of God, or it may be many, complete in all grandeur and beauty, and representing fitly the great ideas, and glorious populations, and high creative powers of a universal Christian age."[58]

Conclusion:

Since beginning this paper I have learned that two great-granddaughters of Horace Bushnell are members of the Unification Church. It would be foolish, of course, to conclude that he was some kind of embryonic nineteenth century Unificationist. His high christology alone would be enough to distinguish him from the messianic hopes of the Unificationists. But he would be the first to agree that someone's personality and ideas do bear fruit in later generations. In any case, it seems evident that some of the theological conclusions reached by Bushnell are shared by the theology of the Unification movement.

FOOTNOTES

[1]Horace Bushnell, *Nature and the Supernatural* (New York: Scribner's, 1858), p. 70.

[2]Bushnell, *Nature and the Supernatural*, p. 71.

[3]Bushnell, *Nature and the Supernatural*, p. 80

[4]Bushnell, *Nature and the Supernatural*, p. 109

[5]Horace Bushnell, *The Spirit in Man* (New York: Scribner's, 1903), p. 248.

[6]Bushnell, *Nature and the Supernatural*, p. 123.

[7]Horace Bushnell, *Christian Nurture* (New Haven: Yale University Press, 1960).

[8]Bushnell, *Nature and the Supernatural*, p. 128.

[9]*Divine Principle*, (Washington: Holy Spirit Association for the Unification of World Christianity, 1973), pp. 206-7.

[10]*Divine Principle*, pp. 210-11.

[11]*Divine Principle*, pp. 217-18.

[12]Horace Bushnell, *Sermons on Living Subjects* (New York: Scribner's, 1892), p. 454.

[13]Horace Bushnell, *God in Christ* (New York: Scribner's, 1887), p. 208.

[14]Bushnell, *The Spirit in Man*, p. 49.

[15]Chung Hwan Kwak, *Outline of the Principle, Level 4* (New York: Holy Spirit Association for the Unification of World Christianity, 1980), p. 59.

[16]*Outline of the Principle*, p. 107.

[17]Horace Bushnell, *The Vicarious Sacrifice* (New York: Scribner's, 1877), p. 90.

[18]Bushnell, *God in Christ*, p. 194.

[19]Bushnell, *God in Christ*, p. 201.

[20]Horace Bushnell, *Sermons for the New Life* (New York: Scribner's, 1889), p. 354.

[21]Bushnell, *Sermons for the New Life*, p. 355.

[22]Bushnell, *Sermons for the New Life*, p. 407.

[23]Bushnell, *The Vicarious Sacrifice*, p. 32.

[24]Bushnell, *The Vicarious Sacrifice*, p. 111.

[25]Bushnell, *The Vicarious Sacrifice*, p. 164.

[26]*Divine Principle*, p. 52.

[27]*Divine Principle*, p. 39.

[28]Horace Bushnell, *Building Eras in Religion* (New York: Scribner's, 1881), p. 174.

[29]Bushnell, *Christian Nurture*, p. 74.

[30]Bushnell, *Christian Nurture*, p. 199.

[31]Bushnell, *Christian Nurture*, p. 201.

[32]Bushnell, *Christian Nurture*, p. 4.

[33]Bushnell, *Christian Nurture*, p. 13.

[34]Bushnell, *Nature and the Supernatural*, pp. 122-23.

[35]Bushnell, *Christian Nurture*, p. 183.

[36]Bushnell, *Christian Nurture*, p. 93-94.

[37]Horace Bushnell, *Moral Uses of Dark Things* (New York: Scribner's, 1893), p. 151.

[38]*Outline of the Principle*, pp. 28-30.

[39]*Divine Principle*, pp. 91-92.

[40]Bushnell, *Christian Nurture*, p. 188.

[41]Bushnell, *Nature and the Supernatural*, p. 183.

[42]Bushnell, *Sermons for the New Life*, p. 223.

[43]Bushnell, *Sermons for the New Life*, p. 94.

[44]*Outline of the Principle*, p. 29.

[45]*Outline of the Principle*, pp. 28-29.

[46]Bushnell, *Building Eras in Religion*, p. 391.

[47]Bushnell, *God in Christ*, pp. 323-24.

[48]Bushnell, *Building Eras in Religion*, p. 393.

[49]Bushnell, *Building Eras in Religion*, p. 104.

[50]Horace Bushnell, *Work and Play* (New York: Scribner's, 1883), p. 164.

[51]Bushnell, *Work and Play*, p. 164.

[52]Bushnell, *Work and Play*, p. 165.

[53]Bushnell, *Nature and the Supernatural*, p. 283.

[54]Bushnell, *Christian Nurture*, p. 94.

[55]Bushnell, *Christian Nurture*, pp. 174-75.

[56]Bushnell, *Christian Nurture*, p. 173.

[57]Bushnell, *Work and Play*, pp. 39-40.

[58]Bushnell, *Building Eras in Religion*, p. 34.

The New Religions and the Second Naiveté: Beyond Demystification and Demythologization

Frank K. Flinn

In *The Symbolism of Evil* Paul Ricoeur remarks that the "primitive naiveté" which issues from the "immediacy of belief" has been "irremediably lost." The immediacy of belief associated with the first naiveté is no longer accessible to moderns who have passed through the critical furnaces of demystification and demythologization. Faith is accessible to us only through interpretation of past texts and traditions. This accounts for the ascendancy of hermeneutics in the sacred sciences. It is only in passing through the forge of critical consciousness, Ricoeur claims, that we can approach a mediate faith and a "second naiveté."[1]

Yet there exists no general hermeneutic for the recovery of faith. Ricoeur detects two conflicting currents in modern hermeneutics. He encapsulates this conflict in the sentence: "Thus idols must die—so that symbols may live."[2] Ricoeur calls the first mode of hermeneutics the "hermeneutics of suspicion." It is dedicated to the reduction of the illusions and idols of false consciousness with which the human species is beset. The hermeneutics of suspicion is associated with the demystifying critiques of Marx, Nietzsche and Freud. By reducing the symbolism of religious representation to technical signs this troika of demystifiers sought to unmask religion as the opium of the people, the *ressentiment* of the masses, and as systematic illusion. The second mode of interpretation Ricoeur calls the "hermeneutics of the restoration of meaning." In this second mode there is the attempt to approach again the region of the Sacred through a phenomenology of symbol. This mode is identified with the interpretative work of Rudolph Otto, Gerhardus van de Leeuw and Mircea Eliade. Ricoeur's later work in hermeneutics is devoted to the mediation of the conflict in interpretations.

Besides the distinction between destructive and restorative hermencutics, Ricoeur also distinguished between demystification and demythologization.[3] Demystification is the critique of religious representation arising from outside the domain of the sacred sciences, e.g., philosophy, economics, psychology. Demythologization is the critique of religion arising from within the sacred sciences themselves. Ricoeur's typology of the critique of the Sacred is in need of amplification and deepening. The hermeneutics of suspicion was a long time arriving.

The critique of naive consciousness and unproblematic faith is coterminous with the rise of modernity. Modernity has twin tap roots, one anchored in the Reformation and the other in modern experimental science. It is imperative to recollect the steps along the route to the hermeneutics of suspicion.

From De-allegorization to Demythologization

De-allegorization. The Reformation commences with the reduction of the medieval fourfold sense of scripture (the literal, the allegorical, the moral and the anagogical) to the literal, i.e., the historical, sense. The power of medieval exegesis was its ability to provide symbols of immediacy by which human existence would be imagined and life could be lived. Nowhere do we discover this power more fully expressed than in the medieval cathedral. Emile Mâle has described medieval art as a scriptural art.[4] The building blocks of the medieval cathedral were not stones and beams but the typologies and allegories derived from scripture and tradition. The medieval cathedral was a symbolic calculus for the *interpretatio naturæ et historiæ* within the universal themes of Creation, Fall, Redemption and Last Judgment.

The virtue of medieval exegesis, however, concealed a vice. The web of typologies and allegorizations would both surpass and pass by the plainness and directness of the primary meaning, the literal sense, in a cloud of false explications and rationalizations. The weakness to which allegory was prone was the conviction that the true meaning, the hidden philosophical meaning, lay either behind or above the literal sense. Thus the letter was understood to be a false disguise of the spiritual sense intended to deceive the uninitiated. We can see this type of allegorization, for example, in Philo Judæus' transposition of the story of the Fall in Neo-Platonic psychology: Adam = terrestrial mind; Eve = sensation; Serpent = pleasure. Whatever else may be said about this speculative transposition, it de-texturizes the story itself and detours around the fundamental ambiguity of the two accounts of creation: the paradox of finding oneself having been created good yet inclined toward evil. In reality, the allegory dislocates the authentic paradox and replaces it with a false one: a "good" spirit housed in an "evil" body.

The obscurantizations of medieval allegory motivated the reformational "return to the Letter" and the establishment of the principle that scripture interprets itself (*scriptura suæ ipsius interpres*). There may be obscure passages in scripture, Luther argued, but the obscurity is due to our own linguistic and grammatical ignorance and not to any obscurity in the content of scripture itself.[5] Whatever had been concealed in former times was now revealed in Christ. Rather than resorting to such allegorical handbooks as Dionysius Areopagiticus' *Ecclesiastica Hierarchia* or Gulielmus Durandus *Rationale Divinorum Officum*, Luther recommends consulting other places in scripture where the meaning is plain and clear.

While avoiding the danger of phantasmagoric allegorization, the Protestant principle of scriptural interpretation ran other risks. What was one to think when the literal sense itself was symbolic and ambiguous? Then, too, christological exegesis is something more than a "literal" reading of the text and had the tendency to collapse the meaning of the Old Testament into the New in a Law/Gospel dialectic. And the stress on the "plain style" of interpretation opened the path to the banal moralization of the text, such as the Puritan sermonizing of The Parable of the Sower in order to get the congregation to plant more potatoes for a bigger harvest.[6] Finally, the principle that *scriptura suæ ipsius interpres* carried with it the implication that scripture was no longer sufficient for the interpretation of the Books of Nature and History but simply rebounded back onto itself.

De-idolization. Luther's de-allegorization of scripture was soon to be accompanied by Bacon's de-idolization of the Book of Nature. Bacon names the idols as those of the Tribe (human nature), the Cave (individual perception), the Market Place (language) and the Theatre (ancient philosophy which emphasized contemplation over action).[7] As Luther sought to sweep away the allegories which obscure the plain sense of scripture, so Bacon sought to smash the idols which impede mankind from re-assuming "empire over nature." The principle of the "return to the letter" dovetails neatly with the Baconian principle of the "return to things themselves" (*ipsissimæ res*).[8] The vacuum created by the principle that nature interprets itself paved the way for the principle that *natura suæ ipsius interpres*. With a mixture of boldness and caution Bacon ranked the Book of Nature ("the book of God's works") on a par with the Book of Scripture as a kind of "second Scripture."[9]

The parallel between Luther and Bacon, however, needs to be qualified. For Luther the Fall meant the corruption of mankind by sin. For Bacon it meant the loss of knowledge and power. Like the modern thinkers who followed him, Bacon underestimated the effects of the Fall and believed that mankind could refurbish the image of God by wresting power from nature through the applied arts. Bacon stands at the midway point in the great hermeneutical reversal of modernity. The new "active science" was to overfill the vacuum left by the principle that scripture interprets itself. Henceforth the interpretation of nature became the criterion for the interpretation of scripture. This is reflected in Spinoza's statement that "the method of interpreting Scripture does not differ widely from the method of interpreting nature—in fact, it is almost the same."[10] Under the demystifying gaze of modern "higher criticism," myth was separated from history, miracles from the laws of nature, and symbolic language from the description of "reality." This led to the second wave of modernity, the disenchantment of the world.

Disenchantment. The phrase die Entzauberung der Welt was made famous by Max Weber and popularized by Harvey Cox in The Secular City. Weber took the phrase from Friedrich Schiller.[11] The word Entzauberung can be translated as "demagification" or "desorcerization" as well as "disenchantment." In the enchanted universe there existed a reality apart from human interest. The world was represented as a "living cosmion" which provided consciousness with symbolic links between the rhythms of nature and human existence. This living cosmion vanished with the rise of modern science which deciphered nature into a system of calculable forces. The forces could be manipulated and transformed to human purposes. In Bacon's words, nature could be put "under constraint and vexed...forced out of her natural course, and squeezed and molded."[12] Thus the living cosmion was disenchanted. In its place was the mechanical cosmos in which nature was reduced to "object." Even the human body, as Hegel was to notice later, appeared in the form of an animated tool.

In disenchantment the world lost its narrativity. The Baconian interpretation naturæ reduced the natural order to an array of "instances" which could be codified and turned into a means of production. The new active science dispelled the world of numina along with such lesser genii as sprites, elves and goblins, but it also took away those sensuous symbolic links whereby human existence could be bonded to the being of the world. This was the beginning of the "fact/value" distinction and that peculiar affliction of late modernity which elsewhere I have called "inner-worldly gnosticism."[13] In the "other-worldly gnosticism" known to the historians of early Christianity, Creation, especially the material creation, was seen as the bungled handiwork of a malevolent Demiurge. The aim of salvation through gnosis was to escape the homelessness of time and the rootlessness of space by a leap into the everlasting abode of the "true Self." In inner-worldly gnosticism there are no cosmic exits and "nature" is not the handiwork of a Demiurge but an accidental conglomeration of matter which is indifferent to human purpose. Nature is not so much evil as "neutral." The "facts" of objective reality are "indifferent" to the "values" the subject arbitrarily bestows upon them. "Facts" are beyond good and evil; they are "value-free." In the disenchanted universe the "facts" no longer present clues for the imaginative representation of existence as story but offer instead ciphers of power for the mastery of human and non-human existence.

Demythification and Demystification. The paradox lying beneath the disenchantment of the world was that, as moderns took ever greater "dominion" over the earth, the physical world became objectivized, factualized and rationalized. The meaning, purpose and finality of the whole evaporated as human "goals" and "values" loomed larger. The humanization of the world, according to the thinkers of late modernity, meant also its rationalization. With the Hegelian and Marxist projects of demythification and demystification, the hermeneutics of suspicion was broadened to include the hermeneutic of history or, perhaps more accurately, the broadening of suspicion implied that history itself was the hermeneutic.

For Hegel, mythical consciousness is alienated consciousness. The rational concept first dwells in the "limitless wealth of forms, appearances and configurations" of the variegated rind of myth.[14] In order for the *Geist* (which is neither the *pneuma* of the New Testament writers, nor the *psyche* of the Greek philosophers, but "subject") to become at home with itself, to become consiousness which is both in itself and for itself, it must shuck off, peel away, and enucleate (*enthüllen*) once-for-all the mystical rind. The alienation engendered by mythical consciousness is overcome only through rational historical action. Nature as alien object is overcome through work, which, in turn, leads to the overcoming of the Master-Slave alienation and to political emancipation. Finally, the divine-human alienation (god as Stranger or Other) is overcome through the acquisition of immanent absolute knowledge. Hegel saw the historical process as one of progressive rationalization and secularization. The Protestant principle, for example, represented both the Christianization of the *sæculum* and the secularization of Christianity.[15] The transition from the alienation of mythical consciousness to reconciled consciousness is refracted in the transition from classical epic (the hero) to the novel (the bourgeois worker) and from poetry to prose.[16] The modern representation of the world is a prosaic representation.

Marx advances upon Hegel's critique of mythical consciousness on two fronts. First, Marx claims that the material conditions of existence are not the expression of the Idea but quite the reverse. The Idea, particularly the idea clothed in religious representation, is often a veil masking the intolerable conditions of alienation. Marx subsumes the critique of religious representation under ideology critique. Religious suffering, for example, is the "expression of real suffering," but religion also serves as "the opium of the people."[17] The authentic religious sigh becomes deflected and mystified when the protest of the afflicted is transposed into an imaginary "Heaven" where all wrongs will be righted. Secondly, Marx's critique of "holy" illusions lays the groundwork for the critique of the "unholy" or secular illusions in law, politics and economics. For example, Marx exposed the 19th Century monetary system as a fetishistic pseudo-religion in which money functioned as an "actual god" by which human relationships were reduced to a material commodity relationship.[18]

In the *Republic* Plato subjected myth and poetry to the critique of the *logos*. The Platonic critique, however, was not aimed at the abrogation of mythic consciousness but only at its purgation (*katharsis*). Demythification and demystification, by contrast, have as their intended purpose the annulment of myth and symbol in the pursuit of rational consciousness. Though Hegel and Marx stripped religious representation of its ideological links with the structures of alienation, domination and submission, the future held in store only greater bureaucratization and rationalization of life and world.

Disillusionment and Decipherment. By historical reckoning disillusionment and decipherment follow demythification and demystification. Structurally speaking, they relate to disenchantment. The disenchantment of the world as object was the prelude to the disenchantment of the world as subject. The fortress of the Ego, initially so confident of its inwardness in faith (Luther) and its certainty in doubt (Descartes), succumbed to the distressing critiques of Nietzsche and Freud.

In Nietzsche's critique of religious representation, the hermeneutics of suspicion attains its full destructive force. Nietzsche unmasks
the religious motive as the revenge of the weak against the strong, the
apotheosis of lower herd instincts (Christianity as Platonism for the
masses) and the *ressentiment* against the becomingness of the world.[19] For
Nietzsche, all goals ("ideals") have no ontological connection with the
world but issue from human evaluation; all evaluations come from
self-overcoming and all self-overcoming is reducible to the will-to-
power. In particular, Nietzsche unveils Christianity as the devaluation
of the noble religion of the strong (the Greeks) and the creator of
world-negating values which vitiate the affirmation of natural life "by
inventing *another* world."[20] Where Marx stood for a critique of religious consciousness from the left, Nietzsche stands for the critique
from the right.

Nietzsche uncovered the naked "self" and Freud proceeded to
dismantle that "self" from within in his decipherment of the psychic
life into an economy of drives (Unconscious, Conscious, Preconscious)
or, later, into a topography of competing domains (Id, Ego, Superego).
The apparent autonomy of the conscious Ego was dethroned, and the
decipherment of dreams uncovered an infinitude of desire attached
to the indestructible narcissism of the child's wish for fulfillment.
Freud's critique of religious representation is introduced in the context of infantile wish-fulfillment. Religion is systematic illusion (Freud
distinguished illusion from both delusion and error) which never rises
above the imperialism of the infantile wish. Naive religion is, for
Freud, religion proper and any softening of the primal guilt associated
with the timeless murder of the primordial father with notions of
Providence or "oceanic feeling" of oneness with the universe is but
secondary distortion and illusion.[21] The analysis of religious imagery
suffers the same fate as the analysis of dream imagery.

Demythologization. Demythologization represents the critique of
religious representation from within the sphere of faith itself. Given
the destructiveness of the hermeneutics of suspicion, demythologization is the attempt to recover a critical faith in post-modernity.

It rests on the twin foundations of Barth's critical theology and Bultmann's demythologizing hermeneutic. With these two enter-prises there is a recognition that one cannot return to the first naiveté of religious representation.

According to Barth, critical faith arises when fallen humanity encounters the KRISIS of God in the proclamation of the Gospel (*kerygma*). The KRISIS is dialectical: a "No" to the old Adam and human achievement and a "Yes" to the new humanity bestowed by God in Christ. Following Kierkegaard, Barth distinguishes radically between faith and religion. Faith is the encounter with God as wholly other. It is in no way grounded on our experience or capacity to represent the divine. Religion, on the other hand, is "the supreme possibility of all human possibilities."[22] As such, it can fall into the idolatry to which all human institutions are prone. Critical faith unmasks religion as a narcotic. Critical faith, or, better, faith under KRISIS, is not a tangible reality within human grasp but faith in faith itself.

Bultmann's demythologization builds upon Barth's notion of critical faith. As Hegel and Marx sought to extract the rational kernel from the mythical rind of consciousness, so Bultmann seeks to extricate the nucleus of faith—the kerygmatic event of the Word of God addressed to each person in his or her existential depth—from the mythological representation in which it was originally embedded. Demythologization is *not* an accommodation of the scriptures to the scientific presuppositions of modern consciousness. Rather, it is the attempt to enucleate the authentic *skandalon* of the biblical Summons to moderns in spite of their adherence to a modern scientific world view.[23] Through demythologization the cultural vehicle of mytholog-ical language in which the kerygma was first embedded is revealed as a false scandal. The real stumbling block, according to Bultmann, is the word of the cross.

The Recovery of Symbol: The Second Naiveté

The path which has led from de-allegorization to demythologiza-tion has, I believe, irretrievably removed the function of religious language as scientific explication. The symbols and myths (or stories) through which religious discourse achieves its aims can only appear as a science-*manqué* from the perspective of a modern scientific world view. However, this destructive consequence has a restorative side. If religious discourse is not science-minus, then perhaps it is poetry-plus. Paul Tillich has suggested that Bultmann's project of demythologization ought to be called deliteralization for it recovers for us the function of religious languages as symbolic representation.[24]

Sign vs. Symbol. Scientific discourse operates through the use of signs which are fixed in intentions, transparent in meaning and stable throughout argumentation. Signs allow for the organization of a field of experience of what Kant calls the schematism. In logical discourse equivocation in the use of the sign would be intolerable. Yet in order to achieve their purpose, signs must abstract from the existential thickness of existence. Symbols proceed along a different route. Symbols arise when a primary meaning ("the letter") gives rise to another meaning ("the spirit") which is yet bound to the first. Thus symbols are equivocal. Ricoeur and Victor Turner have discussed how symbols have double meanings which link sensuousness with normativity and the rich texture of existence with ultimate meaning.[25] The equivocation of symbols, however, does not arise through a default of religious discourse but through the surplus of meaning which symbols embody. Symbolic discourse says more than can be said in logical discourse.

The double-vector quality of symbols, however, necessitates a hermeneutic of suspicion. Between the primary and secondary meaning there can emerge all sorts of distortions and falsifications. From this perspective, symbolic discourse is in need of logical discourse which "dis-implicates" the primary symbolism from false secondary elaborations. But this takes place in and through symbolic discourse itself. Here the example of Second Isaiah is instructive. In the complex and rich language of this prophet we encounter both the extreme of iconoclasm and destruction of false idols. (Is. 44:1 ff.) and yet the recrudescence of mythic symbols of Creation and Exodus interwoven with inverted myths of the Ancient Near East, vignettes from everyday life and historical events surrounding the reign of Cyrus. But, it should be pointed out, in Second Isaiah the very moment of the destruction of false idols of consciousness (religious symbols which have sedimentized into graspable idols of the Wholly Other) is also the moment of resymbolization. In the critical consciousness of modernity, on the other hand, the reduction of meaning to the transparency of the technical sign has created a crisis in symbolization.

The Technical Sign. Modernity has terminated in what many have called the technological society. By technology I mean the *techně* (art, craft, making, doing) and *logos* (word, reason, rationale, knowing).[26] Though the term is derived from the Greek, it is important to point out that the ancient Greeks would have never joined these two words, i.e., they never would have placed knowing on the same level with doing. The word "technology" is a neologism which arose sometime early in the 17th Century. There is no doubt that technology has given moderns great mastery over both non-human and human nature. Yet the very mastery over our external and internal environment has generated a crisis in symbolization. Why is this so?

The very power of technological mastery conceals a darkness. The technical sign, to which all has been reduced, *homogenizes* the heterogenous. Within this homogenization humans are constrained to envision their lives in terms of inflation rates, statistical averages, economic projections, etc. The very transparency of the modes of measurement demands that people abstract from the very texture of their existence. Secondly, the technical sign is *totalizing.* Nothing is immune from its analytic mastery—religion, art, sexuality, etc. Thirdly, the technical sign *rationalizes* existence, i.e., it tends to reduce everything to a means-ends criterion of efficiency. In *Toward a Rational Society* Jürgen Habermas has argued that technology possesses a "glassy background ideology"[27] which tends to close down the transmission of meaning (the hermeneutical function). Technical signs facilitate the making of "decisions" but they do not necessarily engender "meaning," which is carried by communities of people who are in dialogue with one another. The technical sign is "monologic."

Recovery of Symbol. This is the point where I see the new religious movements entering in. I believe that one of the unrecognized aspects of new religious movements is their recovery of life as story, and in order to tell that story one needs recourse to symbols. The very ascendancy of the technical sign has meant that human existence has taken on a metonymic thinness and prosaic meaninglessness. The new religious movements represent not simply the search for the Sacred but also the quest for metaphoric richness by which the story of life can be symbolized and lived out. Furthermore, the recovery of symbol takes place within the context of communities. The technological society thrives best on the isolated individual—the narcissistic "consumer"—and the aloof, abstract corporate bureaucracy. It is no wonder that technological mastery has wreaked havoc on the intermediate institutions such as family, church, voluntary associations, etc. Thus the search for symbol is identical with the search for community, for the community is the proper locus of symbolic dialogue about the meaning of life and death.

The very success of the technical sign has produced a crisis in symbolization. Although computers can do marvelous things, they cannot tell stories about human life. All they can do is process information and information is constituted by endless seriality. Information has no beginning, no middle and no end. In order to tell the story of life, one needs symbols which unite the concrete sensuousness and relatedness of existence with images of a universal destiny. In a curious way, our situation parallels that of the Roman Empire in the First Century A.D. As the empire closed back on itself and sought to manage the population, a kind of meaninglessness set in. It was at this time that we find the spread of the new religious movements—the mystery religions, Mithraism, the cult of Isis, along with Judaism and Christianity. I think one of the principal reasons for the phenomenal spread of Christianity is that it had concrete stories to tell, stories like those about Adam and Eve, Abraham, Moses, David and Jonah. Through these symbolic stories people could find the mirrors of their own lives. The concrete stories were bound up with the universal themes of the Creation, the Fall, the Redemption and the Last

Judgment. Something similar, I suggest, is happening in the new religious movements.

Facts, data sheets, economic projections, etc., are not the material with which human life can be symbolized. They may be a part of existence in the modern world, but they cannot give life a meaning. Ultimate and sacred symbols are not just frosting on the cake. Yet the unspoken imperative of the technological society is for us to disenchant ourselves of our visions of the Good, to de-idolize the past, to decode and decipher our dreams into neurological forces, to disillusion ourselves of the religious dimension, to demystify the process of society and even to demythologize our sacred books. I do not think that we moderns can escape the consequences of the hermeneutics of suspicion. At the same time, none of us should be surprised that from within the ascesis of meaning in which modernity has terminated, the phoenix of the symbol rises from the ashes. It is in times like these that some perceive that the symbols of the Sacred, illusion though they be, are still necessary illusions. The recovery of symbol in the new religious movements represents a search for what Ricoeur calls the "second naiveté" or "the postcritical equivalent of the pre-critical hierophany."[28]

If I apply some of these thoughts to Unification theology, I would say first and foremost that *Divine Principle* reconstitutes the symbolic narrativity of the messianic story. This narrativity is not simply a succession of events attached arbitrarily to a series of dates but a pattern or plot—or what Aristotle calls a *mythos* (*Poetics* 1450a 37)—which has a beginning, a middle, and an end. The parts of a plot are not related to one another episodically, i.e., on a foundation of mechanical seriality. Aristotle calls the plot the "soul" of the story whereby the beginning, the middles and the end are related by way of repetition and inversion. One can read the end in the beginning and the beginning in the end. In an earlier essay I compared *Divine Principle* to Milton's *Paradise Lost* and *Paradise Regained*.[29] Both works might be called *theological epics*. They do in words what the medieval cathedral did in stone by encompassing the story of Creation, Redemption and Glorification (Restoration) within a symbolic whole.

Divine Principle claims to have uncovered the mythos of Heilsgeschichte by uncovering the original purpose of Creation (DP, pp. 41-46). From the structural aspect of the plot, the Fall of humanity constitutes a deflection from the original purpose of Creation. The thematic motive of history—in Aristotle's term, the dianoia—is the restoration of the original principle of Creation which is defined as the Kingdom of God on Earth. The path to restoration is marked by repeated attempts by "central figures" and repeated failures (DP, p. 56). The understanding of history in Divine Principle is neither linear nor cyclic. Rather history happens on the model of a gyre or spiral with greater and greater intensification in messianic expectation. Thus it would be erroneous, I believe, to interpret the "central figures" and "periods of time-identity" (DP, pp. 45-47) as flat cyclic repetitions on the model of the Greek kykloi or the Hindu jugas. Rather, Divine Principle unfolds the messianic story in a way that used to be called typological. Today typological exegesis has gone out of fashion but in former times typology was the mode whereby the greatest minds discovered the truth and unity of the Bible and the coincidence between the truth of the Bible and the truths of nature and history. Figures and types—today we would say symbols—were routes to the truth. "The type," wrote Pascal, "is made according to the truth; and the truth is recognized according to the type."[30] Thus Adam is a type for Christ (the antitype of which the type is the foreshadowing).

An innovation in Divine Principle is that it reads the type-antitype formula both forwards and backwards. Adam is not only a fore-shadowing of the Christ. The Christ is also a recapitulation of the original Adam (and Eve). Thus Unification Christology is modified by its "Adam/Eve-ology." Futhermore Christology and "Adam/Eve-ology" both articulate and are articulated by Divine Principle's Adventology, i.e., the teachings pertaining to the Lord of the Second Advent, the restored Family and the True Parents. In this way the teaching about the beginning (the original Ideal Family) and about the end (the True Parents) modify Unificationist Christology. The Christ's mission was to restore the broken relationship between man and woman and humans and God by taking a Bride and raising children in a God-centered family. From this aspect, the mission of Jesus was incomplete. Certain Christian critics of Unification theology object that, since *Divine Principle* teaches that Jesus failed in his mission, Unification "cannot be regarded as Christian."[31] Against this objection, two things may be said. First, *Divine Principle* does not precisely say that Jesus failed but, rather, that the will of God for the full spiritual and physical restoration of humanity was failed by the disbelief of the people in Jesus (DP, p. 196). Second, *Divine Principle* claims that Jesus and the Holy Spirit did fulfill their mission of "spiritual True Parents" (DP, p. 217). It remains the role of the Lord of the Second Advent and his Bride to bring the physical restoration in line with the spiritual restoration already fulfilled by Jesus and the Holy Spirit.

These criticisms of Unification theology, however, come from a viewpoint that places priority on doctrine whereas the deep structure of *Divine Principle* reveals a typological *mythos* or symbolic narrative. Before Unification is put through the acid bath of conventional orthodoxy, I think it is incumbent upon the critic to recognize the fundamental symbolic structure of *Divine Principle*. Doctrinally speaking, Unificationism is a two-article theology (Creation/Restoration).[32] This doctrine, however, is encoded in the symbolic narrative about the coming of the Messiah. Originally, Adam and Eve were to be, so to speak, their own messiahs. In the Fall they disrupted the process of the three Blessings both on the physical and spiritual levels. Through Jesus and the Holy Spirit the spiritual dimension was restored but not the physical. Finally, the full restoration is brought about by the Lord of the Second Advent and his Bride. The bare bones of this symbolic structure can be diagrammed thus:

		ADAM/EVE	JESUS/SPIRIT	LORD/BRIDE	
CREATION	physical	−	−	+	RESTORATION
	spiritual	−	+	+	

Whatever else may be said about *Divine Principle*, I think that, as a typological *mythos* for post-modernity, it presents a consistent and motivating symbolic structure for the adherents of the Unification

Church. Many researchers into Unificationism overlook the symbolic and narrative dimension to conversion to the movement. Most believers will tell you that they were first convinced of the truth of Unification after hearing the Fall of Man lecture based on *Divine Principle*. In other words, many have come to a second naiveté in, through and by a story that claims to uncover the fundamental human predicament and holds forth a solution for the restoration of the world.

FOOTNOTES

[1]Paul Ricoeur, *The Symbolism of Evil*, trans. Emerson Buchanan (Boston: Beacon, 1967), p. 351.

[2]Paul Ricoeur, *Freud and Philosophy: An Essay on Interpretation*, trans. Denis Savage (New Haven: Yale University Press, 1970), p. 531.

[3]Paul Ricoeur, *The Philosophy of Paul Ricoeur*, ed. Charles E. Reagan and David Stewart (Boston: Beacon, 1978), pp. 213-22.

[4]Emile Mâle, *The Gothic Image: Religious Art in France of the Thirteenth Century*, trans. Dora Nussey (New York: Harper, 1958), pp. 14-22.

[5]Martin Luther, *Bondage of the Will*, in *Martin Luther: Selections from His Writings*, ed., John Dillenberger (New York: Doubleday, 1961), p. 172

[6]Perry Miller, ed., Introduction, *Images or Shadows of Divine Things*, by Jonathan Edwards, (New Haven: Yale University Press, 1948), pp. 15ff.

[7]Frances Bacon, *The New Organon and Related Writings*, ed. Fulton H. Anderson (Indianapolis: The Library of Liberal Arts, 1960), pp. 47-60.

[8]Bacon, p. 114.

[9]Bacon, p. 282

[10]Benedict Spinoza, *Theologico-Political Treatise*, trans. R.H. Elwes (New York: Dover, 1951), p. 99.

[11]Max Weber, "Science as a Vocation," in *From Max Weber: Essays in Sociology*, ed. H.H. Gerth and C. Wrights Mills (New York: Oxford University Press, 1958), pp. 139ff.

[12]Bacon, p. 25.

[13]Frank K. Flinn, "George Grant's Critique of Technological Liberalism" (Diss. Univ. of St. Michæl's College, Toronto, 1981), pp. 268ff.

[14]G.F.W. Hegel, Preface, *The Philosophy of Right*, in *The Philosophy of Hegel*, ed. Carl J. Friedrich (New York: Modern Library, 1954), p. 225.

[15]G.F.W. Hegel, The Philosophy of History, trans. J. Sibree (New York: Dover, 1956), pp. 342-45.

[16]G.F.W. Hegel, Aesthetik in Hegels Sämmtliche Werke, ed. H. Glockner (Stuttgart: F. Frommann, 1927-41), III, 341, 395.

[17]Karl Marx, Introduction, "Toward a Critique of Hegel's Philosophy of Law," in Writings of the Young Marx on Philosophy and Society, ed. Lloyd D. Easton and Kurt H. Guddat (New York: Doubleday, 1967), pp. 250-251.

[18]Marx, p. 266.

[19]Cf. esp. Friedrich Nietzsche, Beyond Good and Evil: Prelude to a Philosophy of the Future, trans. R.J. Hollingdale (Harmondsworth: Penguin, 1973), pp. 56-71.

[20]Friedrich Nietzsche, The Anti-Christ, in Twilight of the Idols & The Anti-Christ, trans. R.J. Hollingdale (Harmondsworth: Penguin, 1969), p. 135.

[21]Sigmund Freud, The Future of an Illusion, trans. James Strachey (New York: Norton, 1961), pp. 30-33.

[22]Karl Barth, The Epistle to the Romans, trans. Edwyn C. Hoskyns (London: Oxford Univ. Press, 1968), p. 241.

[23]Rudolph Bultmann, Jesus Christ and Mythology (New York: Scribner's, 1958), p. 36.

[24]Paul Tillich, A History of Christian Thought, ed. Carl E. Braaten (New York: Touchstone, 1968), p. 524.

[25]Ricoeur, Freud and Philosophy, pp. 28-32; Victor Turner, The Forest of Symbols: Aspects of Ndembu Ritual (Ithaca: Cornell Univ. Press, 1967), pp. 27-29.

[26]George P. Grant, English-Speaking Justice, The Josiah Wood Lectures 1974 (Sackeville, New Brunswick: Mt. Allison Univ. Press, 1978), p. 88.

[27]Jürgen Habermas, "Technology and Science as 'Ideology,'" in Toward A Rational Society: Student Protest, Science, and Politics, trans. Jeremy Shapiro (Boston: Beacon, 1971), p. 111.

[28]Ricoeur, The Symbolism of Evil, p. 352.

[29]Frank K. Flinn "Christian Hermeneutics and Unification Theology," in A Time For Consideration: A Scholarly Appraisal of the Unification Church, ed. M. Darrol Bryant and Herbert W. Richardson (New York: Mellen, 1978), pp. 153-56.

[30]Blaise Pascal, Pensèes (Paris: Editions Gallimard, 1936), p. 315.

[31]"A Critique of the Theology of the Unification Church As Set Forth in 'Divine Principle'" (National Council of the Churches of Christ, Faith and Order Commission, June, 1977), p. 5.

[32]Herbert Richardson, "A Lecture to Students at the Unification Theological Seminary in Barrytown, New York," in Bryant and Richardson, pp. 295-98.

The Unification Church
as Metainstitution

Lonnie D. Kliever

For all its sociological acuity and theological alertness, the Unification Church has no clearly developed ecclesiology. One searches in vain for any sustained discussion of the Unification Church as an institution in Divine Principle or in the numerous theological commentaries and conferences devoted to an exposition of Divine Principle. This absence is all the more remarkable since the sociological-theological classification of this religious movement has played such an important role in the religious and political controversy surrounding the Moonies. Crucial issues hinge on whether Unificationism is seen as a Church, a Sect or a Cult, to say nothing of those who portray Unificationism as an economic empire, political movement or international conspiracy masquerading as a religion. How different the whole climate surrounding the Moonies would be if theologians, social scientists, legislators, judges, parents and the public could agree on what kind of religious movement and ecclesiastical organization Unificationism represents.

But such agreement is not likely to be achieved in the near future for at least two reasons. Many of the sociological-theological descriptions of the movement are ideologically motivated. This bias can be seen within and without the Unification movement. Within, the change in name from the "Holy Spirit Association for the Unification of World Christianity" to the "Unification Church" is symptomatic of Unificationist efforts to enter the mainstream of American and European life partly through a process of labeling. The Unificationist pose under certain circumstances as yet another Christian "church" plays fast and loose with sociological if not theological categories. Moreover, Unificationists are quick to deny under other circumstances that they are a "church" at all, insisting rather that they are a movement to unite all religions, Christian and non-Christian alike. More flagrant and pernicious bias can be seen outside the movement in the widespread labeling of Unificationism as a cult, where "cult" is pejoratively defined as a movement which denounces the established social order as totally depraved and evil, seeks a total authoritarian transformation of society and seduces unwary young persons away from institutionalized roles in families, schools and churches in order to absorb them into a "totalistic community" (cf. Enroth, 1977; Stoner and Park, 1977). So long as categories such as "church" and "cult" are used in such self-serving ways, we cannot begin to hope for agreement on what kind of religious movement Unificationism represents and how that movement relates to other religious and cultural institutions.

Beyond such ideological labeling, formidable theoretical obstacles stand in the way of a consensus description of the Unification movement. There simply are no universally accepted typologies of religious organization among social scientists. The simple Church-Sect typology derived from the pioneering work of Max Weber and Ernst Troeltsch continues to be modified and elaborated by social scientists. From H. Richard Niebuhr's extended Sect-Denomination-Church continuum (Niebuhr, 1929), ever increasingly divergent systems of classification have been developed—e.g., J. Milton Yinger's six main types of religious groups: (1) the Universal Church, (2) the Ecclesia, (3) the Denomination, (4) the Established Sect, (5) the Sect, and (6) the Cult (Yinger, 1970); Bryan Wilson's division between (1) Conversionist, (2) Revolutionist, (3) Introversionist, and (4) Manipulationist sects and his further distinctions between (5) Thaumaturgical, (6) Reformist, (7) Utopian and (8) Ritualist sects (Wilson, 1969); Geoffrey Nelson's distinction between "spontaneous" and "permanent" cults and the further division of the latter into permanent local cults, unitary centralized cults and federal centralized cults (Nelson, 1968). This burgeoning literature on types of religious organization, while obviously overlapping at many points, is still moving away from rather than toward consensus classifications and explanations of religious groups.

There are good reasons for this diversity of nomothetic constructs in the social scientific study of religious groups. These constructs were initially developed for the analysis of Central European and North American Christian groups. As social scientists began to cast a wider net to include non-Christian and Christian, ancient and contemporary, Eastern and Western, traditional and syncretistic religious groups, those simpler typologies obviously required modification and elaboration. The ways in which religious groups emerge, stabilize and develop as they interact with other religious and social groups have proven to be both complex and changing. Little wonder that theories of religious organization are so divergent!

Recognizing these reasons for diversity among classificatory schemes of religious organization helps explain why Unificationism is so difficult to classify. The Unification Church is a microcosm of the data of the scientific study of religious groups. Unificationism combines Christian and non-Christian, contemporary and ancient, Western and Eastern, traditional and syncretistic themes in complex and changing ways. As such, Unificationism fails to fall neatly into the prevailing typological categories. This elusiveness and its implications will become more clear if we test Unificationism against the prevailing typological models of religious organization.

I. The Limiting Cases—Church and Mysticism

Though Troeltsch's pioneering classification of religious organization has clearly been superseded, two of his categories may still serve as useful pointers to the limiting cases for any such typology. Commentators often forget that Troeltsch did not offer a binary Church-Sect classification but rather a tripartite Church-Sect-Mysticism scheme (Troeltsch, 1931). "Church" and "Mysticism" are his limiting cases of the sociological development of Christianity.

According to Troeltsch, the Church as a type is a religious group that recognizes the importance and integrity of the secular world. Rather than abandoning or battling the secular world, the Church accepts the main structures and functions of the secular world as penultimate goods. The Church is therefore built on a compromise which ideally extends the Church throughout the culture and absorbs the culture into the Church. Individuals are born into the Church as surely as they are born into the State. Indeed, Church and State are mutually supportive, though quarrels over priorities and prerogatives within this mutuality have been long and often bitter. The Church stabilizes and sanctions the State. The State supports and defends the Church. Going somewhat beyond Troeltsch's description, we may define the Church as "a religious association characterized by (1) a relatively high degree of institutionalization, (2) integration with the social and economic order, (3) a membership recruited on the basis of residence or family, and (4) relatively restrained and routinized participation" (Broom and Selznick, 1977:386).

According to Troeltsch, Mysticism appears when ideas which have hardened into formal worship, abstract doctrine and conventional religiosity are transformed into a purely personal and inward experience. This characterization of mystical religious experience is reminiscent of William James' analysis in terms of ineffability, noetic quality, transiency and passivity (James, 1902). Mysticism is thus essentially individualistic. This highly personal and private religious experience may give rise to the formation of informal groups, but these associations develop no authoritative doctrine or social strategy. On the contrary, they emphasize the importance of individual religious experience, liberty of conscience and otherworldly vision.

Defined in these terms, Unificationism is obviously neither a "Church" nor a "Mysticism," though there are elements and tendencies of each within Unification thought and life. Of course, churches do not spring full blown from the head of Zeus or Christ; nor do mysticisms remain insular and isolated visions of another world wholly separated from this world—sociological facts that Troeltsch overlooked or ignored. Perhaps Unificationism is a religious movement born of the mystical experience of the Rev. Moon and his first associates but now growing toward a church which will indeed be truly one, holy and catholic. But as the Unification Church stands today, he/she is neither a "Church" nor a "Mysticism." But the possibility of such an historical development and the fact of observable changes within the movement suggest alternative classifications of Unificationism.

II. The Presumptive Alternatives—Sect or Cult

For all the typological complexity and variety, most scientific definitions of "Sect" and "Cult" are drawn with reference to Church and Mysticism as the limiting cases. Sect and Cult are more or less stable religious organizations which are neither establishments of traditional religion nor assemblies of private piety. Some social scientists see the Sect and the Cult moving inexorably toward either establishment or dissolution. Others see Sect and Cult as relatively permanent types of religious organization. But whether transient or permanent, most social scientists regard Sect and Cult as distinct and identifiable types of religious organization.

No attention can be given here to the entire literature on the Sect as such. Our purposes can be served, however, by a generic description of Sect that is mindful of the diversity in this literature. The Sect no less than the Church claims a unique legitimation as means of access to truth and salvation, though this means is not invested in a sacerdotal system or hierarchical priesthood. The Sect is a group that repudiates the Church's compromises with the world and withdraws from both the Church and the world in search of purity of rite and dogma. Typically there is a voluntary membership which stresses individual perfection. Sectarian movements always stand in sharp opposition to society though they differ over how that opposition is expressed—whether through chiliastic transformation, ascetic differentiation or revolutionary agitation (Werner Stark, 1967). Thus, the Sect is free from worldly alliances and ecclesiastical hierarchies.

Drawn thus sharply, the organizational problems of religious sects and the conceptual difficulties for a Sect typology are apparent. Ideally, the Sect is a one-generational phenomenon, born of religious dissatisfaction or cultural deprivation. But sects are seldom such short-lived protests. What happens to the sect when children of believers are born, when a clergy replaces lay leaders, when prosperity and respectability are achieved? The sect, of course, takes on a different sociological if not theological character. These shifts are charted in the typological refinements of the Sect noted above and in the development of such additional categories as Denominationalism or Ecumenism as mediating sociological forms on the Church-Sect continuum. Nevertheless, those sects which become fully institutionalized always retain something of their original sense of the gathered community in opposition to the world. Such sectarian iconoclasm and authoritarianism can be perpetuated through many generations.

Defining the category of the Cult confronts us with difficulties and developments of a different kind. The sociological category of the Cult as developed by Howard Becker and Milton Yinger (Becker, 1932; Yinger, 1957) is closely related to Troeltsch's type of Mysticism. For Becker and Yinger, the Cult is a syncretistic movement usually inspired by a charismatic leader and typically centered in mystical experiences. Rodney Stark introduced an important further clarification by noting that cults unlike sects draw their inspiration from other than the primary religion of the culture. They are thus not schismatics concerned with preserving a purer form of the traditional faith but rather pioneers in search of a new form of faith (Rodney Stark, 1965). These various elements can be reduced to three major criteria by which cults are distinguished from other types of religious groups: (1) cults are groups based on mystical, psychic or esoteric experiences, (2) they originate as a fundamental break with the religious traditions of the society in which they arise, and (3) they are more concerned with the problems of individuals than those of social groups (Nelson, 1968).

These criteria allow for a number of historical and structural variations among cults. A cult may originate in the esoteric experiences of a charismatic leader or in the "parallelism of spontaneities" among people having similar experiences (Martin, 1965). Though cults represent a break with the religious traditions of their own society, they may draw their fundamental inspiration from either an existing alien culture or an earlier native tradition. Moreover, such borrowed or retrieved religious concepts may be combined with elements drawn from the dominant religious tradition of the society. Cults may be a loosely organized affair or they may develop into either central-ized or federated organizations. Finally, cults may in time develop into the dominant religion within a society or they may survive for generations as underground or alternative religious traditions. For all these differences, however, the essential feature of the Cult is the break with the dominant religious system. Thus cults are frequently persecuted and they flourish only when the traditional religious system has broken down to the point where that system no longer dominates or legitimates the cultural order.

Though the categories of Sect and Cult have only been briefly described, the difficulties of classifying Unificationism as either type is readily apparent to anyone thoroughly familiar with this complex religious movement. Viewed from a certain perspective, Unificationism is a sect—it has withdrawn from the church and the world in search of purity of rite and dogma; it has a voluntary membership which stresses individual perfection. Viewed from another perspective, Unificationism is a cult—it is based on mystical experience; it does break with the dominant religious tradition; it does focus on the religious problems of individuals. But *which* Unificationism is sectarian or cultic—Korean? Japanese? North American? West coast or East coast? The truth of the matter is that Unificationism has appeared too lately, developed too rapidly, and migrated too widely to be captured in either of these classifications or their multiple permutations. Not that Unificationism is unique and demands a category of its own. It is simply a *modern* religion (Kliever, 1981). Indeed, Unificationism is a quintessentially modern religion and, as such, the typologies devel-oped to classify and explain pre-modern or early modern religious groups simply do not fit. We need new categories for dealing with the institutional forms and societal roles of distinctively modern religious groups such as Unificationism.

III. An Interim Category—The Metainstitution

Both historical and theoretical challenges can be put to the notion that we need new categories for dealing with distinctively modern if not modernized religions. Cannot the received categories of Church, Sect and Cult be refined to include such sociological developments? Obviously, this is the route taken by most social scientists. All three classifications have been variously reformulated to include modernizing tendencies among the religions—e.g., Yinger's subclassifications of the Church (Yinger, 1970); Wilson's elaboration of the typology of the Sect (Wilson, 1966); Roy Wallis' reformulation of the concept of the Cult (Wallis, 1975). Typologies are, of course, heuristic schemes designed to deal with particular problems and thus may be modified when new problems arise. But broadening typologies of Church, Sect or Cult too far weakens their historical and comparative usefulness. Perhaps a wiser course of action is to develop new categories to supplement the Church, Sect, and Cult typologies already in place. For sociological developments currently underway, an interim category like the "Metainstitution" may serve a useful purpose.

Before we examine this interim category more closely, a preliminary question must be addressed. Are religious institutions and religious consciousness, in fact, undergoing dramatic change in modern culture? If Robert Bellah's theory of religious evolution is correct, and I think he is essentially right, then a new stage of religious development is emerging in our time. Bellah traces out a pattern of growing complexity in religion and in society that falls into five distinct stages (Bellah, 1965). These evolutionary stages are not necessarily discontinuous, but in actuality the earlier stages are rapidly spreading throughout today's world.

In Bellah's account, *primitive* religion is that stage where everyday existence and religious life are intimately and fluidly related. There are no special religious roles and organizations separated from ordinary social roles and organizations. Religious roles are fused with other roles because the society is the religious organization. *Archaic* religion represents a growing differentiation between the sacred and the secular though these are not yet separated into a dualism in archaic cultures. Religious institutions are still largely merged with social structures, though the appearance of worshipping cults and priestly classes signal the emergence of a "two-class" system of social and religious structures and symbolizations. *Historic* religion breaks through the cosmological monism and tribal insularity of the earlier stages by affirming a hierarchical and universalistic vision of reality. Though both the heavenly and the earthly worlds are ordered by a sole creator or single principle, clear separations are drawn between the realms of political and priestly leadership and between the roles of the believer and the citizen. *Early modern* religion retains a dualistic separation of this world and the next but collapses all hierarchical structuring of them. Hierarchical, legal and sacramental systems of salvation are supplanted by an emphasis on the direct relation between the individual and God and on worldly life as an expression of that relationship. Though personal autonomy is still severely limited in religious and moral matters, individuals assume increasing control over political and economic affairs. The increasing separation of worldly organizations from ecclesiastical control and legitimation allows more open and voluntaristic forms of religious organization to develop. As such, early modern religion plays a key role in the emergence of the multicentered, self-revising social order that characterizes today's voluntaristic and pluralistic societies. Finally, *modern* religion leaves behind all dualistic conceptions and authoritarian definitions of reality. Indeed, the responsibility for making sense of human existence has shifted more and more to the individual. Modern religious groups exhibit far greater flexibility of organization and fluidity of membership than previously. The role of enforcing standards of doctrine and morality has largely been dropped with the religious group serving as a supportive community for those individuals involved in a search for meaningful solutions to ultimate concerns. The underlying assumption of these modern trends is that culture and personality are endlessly revisable.

Given Bellah's five stages of religious evolution, a case can be made for an evolutionary arrangement of the Church, the Sect and the Cult (Hargrove, 1979: pp.65-67). The Church is the dominant form of religious organization at the historic level of development, the Sect does emerge to prominence in the early modern period, while the Cult seems peculiarly appropriate to the modern stage, though only if the concept of the Cult is reformulated along Wallis' lines as a deviant *and* pluralistic religious movement, only one of a variety of equally legitimate paths to the truth or salvation (Wallis, 1975). But this evolutionary argument finally does not work for two reasons. It requires us to regard the persistence of churches and sects into the modern period of religious development as cultural lag and it obscures the presence of both sects and cults throughout the historic as well as the early modern religious stage. Indeed, all founded religions of the historic period began as cults or as sects (Nelson, 1968: pp.357-58). Only later did Buddhism, Zoroastrianism, Christianity and Islam finally emerge as dominant religious systems of an empire, thereby achieving the sociological status of a Church.

Better that we search for new categories more appropriate to modern organizational forms of religion, without for a moment denying that churches, sects and cults persist in the modern world and are undergoing a process of modernization themselves. Harvey Cox, in his usual inimitable way, has given us a word for such organizational forms—the *metainstitution* (Cox, 1969: pp.93-97). Though Cox speaks of religious metainstitutions more as desiderata than as actualities, his description is suggestive of what in fact· *might* be emerging as a distinctively modern form of religious organization. Cox calls for a special form of flexible institution which exists not for itself but to join the two worlds of "fact and fantasy," or of culture and religion:

> This "metainstitution" must have a number of characteristics. In order to animate fantasy it must cultivate the symbols that opened men to new levels of awareness in the past. It must be in effective touch with the most advanced artistic movement of the day and with historical and transhistorical images of the future. It must teach men to celebrate and fantasize. But above all it must provide a fertile field where new symbols can appear. Since man is body and heart as well as brain, it must include affective and ritual components. Finally, it must be part of the culture in which it lives but sufficiently free so that its fantasies are not pinioned and hamstrung by present expectations (Cox, 1969: pp.94-95).

Admitting that the churches are not such metainstitutions, Cox nevertheless hopes for such a company of "dreamers, seers, servants and jesters." He concludes, "The new church we look for need not come entirely from the churches of today. It certainly will not. It will come, if it comes at all, as a new congeries of elements, some from the churches, some from outside, some from the fertile interstices between. And it will assume a shape we can hardly predict, though we can sometimes see its outlines—in fantasy" (Cox, 1969: pp.96-97).

Is then the Unification Church such a coming metainstitution? That possibility cannot be lightly dismissed. To be sure, the Moonies all too frequently look and act like a church struggling for power, like a sect reaching for purity or like a cult searching for peace. There are strong indications that Unificationism is aging backwards, reaching toward the vanished glory of historic religion's dream of a universal church and a world empire. If these fantasies of universal church and world empire prevail, then Unificationism will either fall between the cracks of passing time or persist as an established sect or a permanent cult. Historic religion's dream of a universal church and a world empire is gone forever.

But there are counterindications that Unificationism may be a part of the "coming metainstitution" that Cox envisions. There are structures and ministries of the Unification Church that have a metainstitutional character—the International Cultural Foundation, the International Conference on the Unity of the Sciences and the fledgling New ERA. What if these are not mere organizational fronts? What if these are the Unification Church, not serving or support-ing its own institutional and doctrinal interests but providing a struc-tural and symbolic context within which diverse individuals and groups, institutions and traditions can freely explore that "infinite-possibility thing" which is modern religion and life!

Could this company of "dreamers, seers, servants and jesters" be a herald of the "new church"? Clearly the game is still too new to call. The odds are that Unificationism will in fact not dare the future as future but rather treat the future as past. But the possibilities *are* there for the Unification Church to pioneer the way toward distinctively modern forms of religious organization.

BIBLIOGRAPHY

Becker, Howard. Revision of L. von Wiese, *Systematic Theology.* New York: Wiley, 1932.

Bellah, Robert. "Religious Evolution." In *Reader in Comparative Religion.* Ed. William A. Lessa and Evan Z. Vogt. New York: Harper & Row, 1965, pp. 36-50.

Broom, Leonard and Philip Selznick. *Sociology.* New York: Harper & Row, 1977.

Cox, Harvey. *The Feast of Fools.* New York: Harper & Row, 1969.

Enroth, Ronald. *Youth, Brainwashing and Extremist Cults.* Grand Rapids, Mich.: Zondervan, 1977.

Hargrove, Barbara. *The Sociology of Religion.* Arlington Heights, Ill.: ALTM, 1979.

James, William. *The Varieties of Religious Experience.* New York: Longmans, Green, 1902.

Kliever, Lonnie D. "Unification Social Hermeneutics: Theocratic or Bureaucratic?" In *Hermeneutics & Horizons: The Shape of the Future.* Ed. Frank K. Flinn. Barrytown, N.Y.: Unification Theological Seminary, Distributed by Rose of Sharon Press, Inc., 1981.

Martin, David. *Pacifism.* London: Routledge, 1965.

Nelson, Goeffrey K. "The Concept of Cult." *Sociological Review,* 16, (1968), pp. 351-62.

Niebuhr, H. Richard. *The Social Sources of Denominationalism.* New York: Meridian, 1957.

Stark, Rodney and Charles Y. Glock. *Religion and Society in Tension.* Chicago: Rand McNally, 1965.

Stark, Werner. *The Sociology of Religion.* New York: Fordham University Press, 1967.

Stoner, Carroll and Jo Anne Parker. *All God's Children.* Philadelphia: Chilton, 1977.

Troeltsch, Ernst. *The Social Teachings of the Christian Churches.* New York: Macmillan, 1931.

Wallis, Roy. "The Cult and Its Transformation." In *Sectarianism.* Ed. Roy Wallis. New York: Wiley, 1975, pp. 35-49.

Wilson, Bryan. *Religion in Secular Society.* Baltimore: Penguin, 1969.

Yinger, J. Milton. *Religion, Society and the Individual.* New York: Macmillan, 1957.

- - - - - - - - - - - -. *The Scientific Study of Religion.* New York: Macmillan, 1970.

Toward an Asianization of Christianity: Demise or Metamorphosis?

T. James Kodera

One of the common charges directed against the Unification Church is the alleged incongruity of "Korean Christianity." The charge stems from the doubt that a teenager in a far corner of the Asiatic continent could receive a revelation in which he was exhorted to take up Jesus' "unfinished task" and to help realize the millenial prayer of the Christians, "Thy kingdom come, thy will be done, on earth as it is in heaven." Such a doubt seems deeply rooted in theological claims and cultural assumptions that have remained scarcely challenged for centuries. There is the Biblical proclamation that God works through history; when taken literally, God unveils his will only in the particularities of his chosen people, the Hebrews. The Reformation claim of self-sufficiency of the Biblical revelation renders the Protestants more adamant than the Catholics to acknowledge the possibility of continuing revelation outside the historic and spatial confines of the biblical people.[1] The puritan and evangelistic missionaries of the nineteenth century West, particularly of North America, lived with the conviction that the white, Christian West was divinely summoned to convert the heathen East from what they regarded as the tyranny of superstition and magic. To confine revelation to historical and cultural particularities is not only to delimit the infinity of divine wisdom but also to disclaim the universality of the very cause that sent forth believing men and women to the farthest regions of the world to lead the "heathens" from darkness to light, from death to life. The white, Christian West has, however, faced the rest of the world as in dire spiritual need, as objects of conversion, but not as a locus in which God may yet reveal Himself as part of his continuing reign over history.

Although the Christians for centuries have sought to read escha-tology unfolding in the ebb and tide of their own history and that of the Hebrews, the turbulent history of the rest of the world has been either condemned as God's judgment or relegated to outside the reaches of God's redemption. In the sixteenth century, the Catholic nations of Europe spread the Gospel to the "heathen" world, but they also colonized the lands of untapped treasures with the might of firearms. Prior to the Pilgrims and the Puritans, North America was discovered by these zealots. The subsequent global expedition of the Protestant nations was no less, if not more, motivated by the incon-gruous amalgam of evangelism and colonialism. Singularly the most pressing cause for turbulence in the non-Christian, non-white parts of the world in the last two centuries is their passionate pursuit of severance from the oppression of western colonial powers. While the prevailing view among the Westerners was to regard it as native rebellions, there were men and women of discerning conscience who found themselves moved by the likes of Mahatma Gandhi and Steven Biko and disturbed by the capacity of their bretheren for savagery in India, Vietnam and South Africa, to name but a few.

In Asia, until the last few decades, normative Christian faith and institution was conceived in western terms. For centuries, the native converts had no access to the highest ecclesiastical offices where standards of Christian belief and conduct were set. It is a fact that in spite of their indigenization policies, the Jesuits did not ordain the natives to priesthood in sixteenth and seventeenth century Japan and elsewhere for reasons unknown other than the suggestion that con-verted, non-white Christians were somehow less legitimate....

This paper explores the possibility of reinterpreting the Chris-tian Gospel in Asian terms in order that not only Christianity may become a viable option for the Asians but also it may once again offer the Westerners a catalyst for a transforming reality, both individually and communally. This paper examines briefly the content and the extent of "Asianization" (a term coined after "westernization"). The purpose is to promote creative thinking and to facilitate ongoing discussion on a number of pivotal questions that need to be raised. Are there common denominators between Christianity and Eastern religious and philosophical heritage? How compatible is human pride with humility which the Christian Gospel exhorts? Why do certain firm religious convictions foster and justify prejudices? What is the meaning of God's working in human history? Are there pre-Christian and extra-Christian factors contributing to the making of "orthodox" Christian teaching? What constitutes Christian faith, hope and love?

* * *

The history of Christian mission, particularly after the sixteenth century, has unfolded a strikingly similar face in different parts of Asia. Before the improved navigation gave the Spaniards and the Portuguese, and later the Dutch and the English, the power to colonize the rest of the world half a millenium ago,[2] there was no fear of the West in the East. Both sides of the world found each other utterly fascinating. Marco Polo's travel on land to China in the thirteenth century, the driving forces behind Christopher Columbus' journey to what he thought was Asia and the whole Silk Road trade illustrate mutual fascination between the East and the West. The Nestorian Christians, the followers of Patriarch Nestorius of Constantinople, who were declared heretical and excommunicated by the ecumenical council in 431, sought refuge in India and China where they were warmly welcomed. After the sixteenth century, however, zealous missionary activities came to be perceived inextricably linked to the far-flung colonialism of the white, Christian nations of the West. The Portuguese Jesuits successfully Christened and colonized the two key ports of the Indian Ocean, Goa and Macao. When Francisco Xavier reached the southern shores of Japan, intending to convert the entire nation from the emperor on down, he enjoyed initial favor. The seed sown by him grew rapidly. By the time Alessandro Valignano, the Italian Jesuit, arrived to become the chief architect of the Japanese mission, there was a flourishing community of some 150,000 Christian converts, mostly in and around the city of Nagasaki. They included many feudal lords who considered their conversion advantageous to their trade with the Portuguese and especially to their military advancement with the superior European weaponry. When the shrewdest and the luckiest among the contending feudal lords succeeded in unifying the war-torn Japan in the late sixteenth century, suddenly there emerged a need to protect the fragile nation from any potential threat, both internal and external. In 1587, Hideyoshi, the Horatio Alger of Japan, ordered the explusion of all Christian missionaries. When disobeyed, six Franciscan missionaries,[3] seventeen Japanese converts and three Japanese novitiates in the Jesuit order, altogether twenty-six, were crucified on a cold winter's morning in 1597 in Nagasaki to show the remaining Christians the fate they, too, might face unless apostatized. A far more systematic and extensive campaign against the followers of the despised teaching of the "foreign devils" was waged under the Tokugawa shogunate. By the mid 1600s, every visible vestige of the mocked religion disappeared, although the most persistent believers, mostly illiterate peasants and fishermen, went into hiding until their descendants were discovered in the mid-nineteenth century.

Why did the feudal rulers of Japan adopt the policy of unrelenting persecution of the Christians? What was their real motive? The more research is done on the subject, the clearer it becomes that if Christianity had not brought with it the aggressive colonialism of the West to Japan, the shoguns would not have feared the missionaries and converts as co-conspirators. Recent historical findings indicate that not only did some of the early Portuguese and Spanish missionaries have colonialist ideas but some even believed that Christianity could take root more quickly through military take-over and recommended as much to their governments.[4]

In China, the Jesuits had considerable success due largely to their extraordinary effort at indigenizing Christianity in native Chinese ideological and cultural terms. The greatest of these pioneers was the Italian, Matteo Ricci, a.k.a. Li Ma-tou (1552-1610), who was gifted with great intellectual acumen in theology, literature and science, combined with engaging personality. Guided by their earlier experiences in India and Japan, Ricci and his followers adopted Chinese cultural mores to a maximum extent, including the donning of a Confucian scholar's gown, while avoiding all open connections with the Portuguese traders in Macao. Instead of preaching they marvelled the Chinese with demonstrations of prisms, clocks and geographical knowledge. Above all, they spoke fluent Mandarin. All these enabled Ricci to represent Christianity as a system of wisdom and ethics comparable to classical Confucianism. Furthermore, Ricci gained access to the innermost circles of the Chinese intelligentsia and court. Ricci received stipend as a scholar from the emperor, while making converts at all levels of the society. Ricci's successors carried on his tradition of indigenization and non-pastoral approach to proselytizing. The German Jesuit, Johannes Adam Schall von Bell (1591-1666), sought to help the Chinese improve their calendar through the application of western astronomy. The Son of Heaven, as the emperor of China was called, took particular interest in the idea because of his responsibility to carry out the "Mandate of Heaven." He needed a calendar that would accurately foretell the position of heavenly bodies and the timing of the seasons. Schall met that need fully, and celebrated his first mass in China in the palace itself. In the meantime, the decay of the Ming regime made the dynasty no longer a worthy focus of loyalty for many Chinese scholars. As a result, they turned to the combination of western science and Christian ethics. The most famous among them was Hsü Kuang-ch'i (Christian name: Paul Hsü, 1562-1633), who, as Grand Secretary, granted missionaries entrée into high official circles. Hsü and Schall helped the Ming court obtain western arms to fight against the surging Manchus. The height of the Jesuit success in China was during the middle decades of the long reign of the mighty emperor K'ang-hsi.[5] The method of sinification as a means of applying Christianity to the concrete realities of China indeed worked. Paul Hsü remarked that Christianity "does away with Buddhism and completes Confucianism." At that time, Buddhism had fallen from favor and Confucianism was on the rise again.

The eclipse of the Jesuit influence was, however, inevitable for one principal reason. Their indigenization efforts were perceived by the purists as going too far. The Jesuits were accused of allowing "pagan worship," referring to their veneration of ancestors before the family altar which was essential to the Chinese way of life. They were charged therefore with allowing the destruction of the original monotheistic character of Christianity. These accusations were reported to the Vatican by the Franciscan and Dominican friars who had a wholly different view on missionary work. Working in Mexico and the Philippines, where the culture was younger and cruder than that of China, providing little resistance to Catholicism, these non-Jesuit missionaries tried to transplant western Christianity on alien lands with no significant change. In the early 1700s, the Vatican scorned the Jesuits.[6] The Yung-chen Emperor, K'ang-hsi's fourth son, turned against the Jesuits and started an active suppression of Christianity in his empire.[7]

The plight of the Jesuits in China illustrates a different tale than that in Japan. Alessandro Valignano's Japanization of Christianity, linking it with devotional Buddhism, enjoyed some success, but the missionaries were summarily expelled from Japan for fear of eventual colonization by the West that had already disturbed the nation with fire arms. The feudal lords of Japan never ceased to view Christianity as a dangerous western influence. In China, on the other hand, the successful indigenization of Christianity was met with strong denunciation by the Vatican on the grounds that indigenized Christianity was not genuine Christianity. Is western, westernized Christianity the normative Christianity? Should it be?

The early history of Christian mission in Korea parallels closely that in Japan. Except for the Nestorians of a millenium or more ago, the Koreans' first encounter with Christianity was, curiously enough, during the Japanese military expedition of Korea in 1592. One of the generals in Hideyoshi's troop was a Jesuit convert named Konishi Yukinaga, a.k.a. Dom Agostinho.[8] After the expedition, the Korean prisoners of war who were taken captive by Hideyoshi converted in large number to Catholicism. Among the martyrs during the anti-Christian campaign in Japan were these Korean converts.[9] The architect of Korean Christianity was an eighteenth century scholarly patrician, Yi Pyok. The Jesuit tracts enthralled him so much that he set aside one day a week for prayer. He convinced his closest friends in the government to sponsor an annual delegation to the Chinese capital to study Christianity. His friend, Yi Seung-Hoon, upon returning from Peking where he was baptized by a missionary, in turn baptized Yi Pyok. This marks the beginning of Korean Christianity. The bishop in Peking, however, admonished the first Korean church for uncanonically appointing priests. Furthermore, the bishop denounced simultaneous ancestor worship, which was an important feature of Korean life and culture under the dominant Confucian influence during the Yi Dynasty (1392-1910). The controversy over ancestor worship precipitated governmental suppression. A noted scholar, together with his nephews, was arrested and beheaded for burning ancestral tablets, while others were imprisoned. The martyrdom provided a powerful incentive for more Koreans to convert to Christianity. Within ten years after Yi Pyok and Yi Seung-Hoon were baptized, there were 4,000 Catholics in Korea. The reason for the systematic suppression of Christianity in eighteenth century Korea was not simply a radical affront to traditional Confucian morality but more critically the fear of colonization by the West. At that time, the Catholic mission in Korea was under the supervision of French priests, and it looked as if the western imperialists were ready to create yet another colony in Asia. The government officials feared that the missionaries were agents of French imperialism in Korea. Such a fear was real in light of the colonization of Indochina (Vietnam, Laos and Cambodia), as well as of North and West Africa.

The threat of colonialism continued in Korea in the late nineteenth and into the twentieth centuries. No longer the white, Christian nations of the West but Japanese imperialism and Russian communism provided the threat. This is precisely why the Protestant mission unfolded a markedly different path from the earlier Catholics in Korea. The Protestant missionaries from the U.S., Canada and Britain worked on behalf of the Koreans in social reform, medical care and education. In 1886, Mary Scranton opened a girls' school, which was to become the largest women's college in the world (Ewha Women's College). The first Protestant missionary, Horace Allen who was also a medical doctor, was called upon to save the life of Prince Min Young-Ik, a conservative statesman who had been severely stabbed during a coup. His successful treatment won the support and confidence of the ruling house because Min was the queen's nephew. At the request of Allen, the king built a government hospital in Seoul. Allen also served as American Consul General and U.S. Minister Plenipotentiary until the Japanese started taking control over Korea in 1905. Meanwhile, in 1887, three years after Allen's arrival, a Presbyterian church was chartered in Seoul. A Methodist church also was established later in the year.

While the chief adversary of Christianity was the nationalists in Japan and China, and also earlier in Korea, Korean nationalism became a strong ally of Protestantism in the late ninteenth century. The continuing alliance accounts for the popularity and stability of Christianity in Korea today. Although born of political circumstances of modern Korea as well as of deliberate efforts of the foreign missionaries, the political indigenization of Protestantism in Korea sets itself apart from the cultural indigenization of Catholicism that was espoused by the Jesuit missionaries in Japan and China in earlier centuries. The marked difference is that the indigenization by the "outsiders," the missionaries, ultimately failed, while the internal indigenization by the native converts themselves took root. Insofar as indigenization is imposed on the natives, assimilation appears not possible.

During the Japanese annexation of Korea between 1910 and 1945, there was a systematic suppression of Christianity and the alliance between Korean nationalism and Christianity strengthened. Marquis Ito Hirobumi of Japan was assassinated in Manchuria in 1909, by a Korean Protestant nationalist. A year earlier in San Francisco, Ito's American adviser was killed by a Korean Catholic. In 1910, an alleged plot to kill the new Governor General was uncovered by the Japanese. Among the thirty-three signers of the 1919 Declaration of Independence, sixteen were Christians and fifteen were followers of Chondogyo, a syncretism of Buddhism, Confucianism and Catholicism. The Japanese military increased its condemnation of the Christian religion, while forcing upon the colonized Koreans the nationalistic brand of Shintoism of Japan.

When the Japanese were defeated in 1945, the Japanese colonialism ended in Korea but the threat of Russian communism became more real than before, particularly in northern Korea. The communists sought to destroy the Christian political organizations, the Social Democratic Party and the Christian Liberal Party, followed by the imprisonment of the clergy, confiscation of the church properties and the execution of some ultra-nationalistic Christians. Samuel Moffett a Presbyterian missionary reports that no less than four hundred ministers were killed. The Korean Christians fled south to unite both as Christians and staunchly anti-communist nationalists. The founder of the Unification Church moved south to Seoul in 1953. The vitality of the Unification movement is deeply rooted in the turbulent history of modern Korea.

The nationalist-Christian alliance in the last two centuries in turn facilitated the indigenization of Christianity at the theological level. The first notable example is Chondogyo, or the Heavenly Way. Ch'oe Cheu-u (1824-64) received a revelation in which he heard the "Sacred Formula":

> May the creative force of the universe be within me in abundant measure. May heaven be with me and every creation will be done. Never forgetting this truth, everything will be known.[10]

From this "Sacred Formula," he derived his basic principle that man and God are one. He articulated the universal monism in the language of Confucian "five essential human relationships," the popular Taoist "unadulterated life," and the Buddhist mind-development. Because Ch'oe saw divinity in every human being, his understanding of Christianity assumed a tone that was more theological and less christological. The centrality of God is only reminiscent of native Korean shamanism, in which Hananim, the Master of the Sky, was worshipped as the supreme deity. Because of its resemblance to the despised Catholicism and its belief in the Master of the Sky as higher than the king, Chondogyo was met with governmental disapproval.

Cho'oe himself was hanged for alleged treason. Chondogyo, however, provided a national pride based upon the importance of self-cultivation, a spiritual discipline long respected in Neo-Confucianism which served as the greatest influence on the traditional Korean intellectuals before the introduction of western thought and religion. Many an uncompromising follower of this syncretic teaching provided relentless support for nationalist causes.

In assessing the syncretic "Korean Christianity," before condemning the idiosyncrasies of the Korean Presbyterian Church or the Unification Church, one must also realize those western elements that were brought to Korea by the missionaries. In the nineteenth century, American missionaries established and taught schools in Korea and included in their curriculum the thinkers who were vital to the American intellectual life such as Horace Bushnell, Dwight Moody, Ralph Waldo Emerson and Henry David Thoreau.[11] The similarities one may find between the nineteenth century American thought and Koreanized Christianity are, in fact, no coincidence at all, when one comes to grips with the historical, cultural and intellectual dynamic of Korea of that century.

* * *

In the turbulent and often tragic history of Christianity in Asia, one may unravel a basic pattern that is woven into the dissimilar background of the three Asian nations. In every case, there is a juxtaposition of two conflicting threads, preservation and expansion. Asian cultures seek to preserve intact their tradition, the ways of thought and life of their ancestors. The impulse of the Christians is, on the other hand, laterally expansive, which is not unrelated to their aspiration for vertical transcendence. The difference is ultimately attributable to the conflict between the instinct of the agrarian people of the monsoon climate and the nomadic people of the desert, among whom the early Christians originate. While the land cultivators of Asia work toward the renewal of life through the mystery of cosmic recycling, the hunters of the Near East find it a matter of survival to conquer untamed territories and peoples. The former seeks stability and continuity, and the latter annexation and hegemony. Recently, Kosuke Koyama remarked in his inaugural address as Professor of Ecumenics and World Christianity at Union Theological Seminary in New York that in the Japanese way of thinking continuity contains discontinuity and cosmology is more comprehensive than eschatology.[12] The expulsion of Christianity from Japan and China is a necessary result of built-in inertia that seeks to preserve the integrity of their respective tradition. That is why the attempts at indigenization by the outsiders were treated as no indigenization at all. Only when indigenization is sought by the natives themselves in cultural as well as political terms as did the Koreans, could there be no collision of the two distinct impulses inherent in Asian and Christian ways. There still remains after diagnosing the historic conflict, however, the unresolved question: is Asianization a demise of Christianity or is it the metamorphosis without which the gospel of Christ could not take root in a land so different from the West, where the first phase of indigenization took place?

FOOTNOTES

[1]Revelatory experiences of some of the most formidable spiritual leaders of the past few centuries have been summarily rejected by mainstream Christian churches, both Catholic and Protestant. Among those declared heretic are: Emanuel Swedenborg, Joseph Smith, Ann Lee and Mary Baker Eddy. See C.S. Braden, *These Also Believe* (New York: Macmillan, 1970).

[2]The compass that enabled long distance journeys on the sea was originally invented by the Chinese. So was the gunpowder that aided the global conquests of the Portuguese and the Spaniards.

[3]The reason why he executed Franciscan missionaries was to avoid interference with over fifty feudal lords in the Nagasaki region who had become Jesuit converts.

[4]For more on the history of Catholic mission to Japan, see Michael Cooper, S.J., *They Came to Japan: An Anthology of European Reports on Japan, 1543-1640* (Berkeley, Calif.: Univ. of California Press, 1965), and George Elison, *Deus Destroyed: the Image of Christianity in Early Modern Japan* (Cambridge, Mass.: Harvard Univ. Press, 1973). For Protestant mission to Japan in the 19th and 20th centuries, which was markedly different in character, see Irwin Scheiner, *Christian Converts and Social Protest in Meiji Japan* (Berkeley, Calif.: Univ. of California Press, 1970).

[5]For K'ang-hsi's upbringing by a Jesuit, see Jonathan D. Spence, *Emperor of China: Self-portrait of K'ang-hsi* (New York: Knopf, 1974).

[6]The Vatican has yet to recognize the descendants of "Clandestine Christians (kakure kirishitan)" who had disguised their Catholic faith under native teachings and practices for over two centuries until they were discovered by Father Bernard Pettijean, a French priest serving the European residents of Nagasaki in the late 19th century.

[7]See John K. Fairbank, Edwin O. Reischauer and Albert M. Craig, *East Asia: Tradition and Transformation* (New York: Houghton Mifflin, 1973), pp. 244-51.

[8]There were three other Christian cohorts of Hideyoshi during the Kyushu Expedition of 1587 that preceeded the Korean Expedition. Among the three was Dom Justo Takayama Ukon.

[9]Public documents from 1614 to 1629 show Korean Catholic martyrs.

[10]Charles Allen Clark, *Religions of Old Korea* (Old Tappan, N.J.: Revell, 1932), pp. 144-72.

[11]See, for example, Thomas McGowan, "Horace Bushnell and the Unification Movement: A Comparison of Theologies," in this volume.

[12]Kosuke Koyama, "Ritual of Limping Dance: A Botanical Observation," *Union Seminary Quarterly Review*, 36 (September, 1981), pp 91-104.

Radical Secularization, the Modern Age and the New Religions

Richard L. Rubenstein

Several months ago I was invited to participate in a symposium to be held at the December 1981 meeting of the American Academy of Religion on the subject of "The Death-of-God Theology Reconsidered." Since I played a visible role in the movement of radical theology, I was pleased to accept. My colleagues in the symposium will be Thomas J.J. Altizer and William Hamilton.

The invitation elicited from me some reflection on the unanticipated direction that my career as a heterodox theologian has taken since the sixties. As some of you may know, I argued in my writings and in public forums that the doctrine of the election of Israel and the belief that God is preeminently the ultimate actor in the drama of history could only be maintained if one regarded the destruction of the European Jews an expression of divine punishment against the Jews. Since I could not so regard the event, I felt compelled to abandon those central tenets of Jewish religious self-interpretation. Had anybody suggested at the time that I would have been willing to adopt a posture of friendship, sympathy and cooperation with a movement whose fundamental energies spring from their faith in God's action in history and the election of the Korean nation as the Third Israel, I would have rejected the idea as utterly beyond the realm of possibility. Nevertheless, that is precisely what has happened. In this paper I propose to share with you one of the principal reasons, though by no means the only one, why this has taken place.

Although it has often been said that I had asserted that "God is dead," I had in fact insisted that no such statement could be made about God and that the term "death of God" was descriptive of the human condition rather than in any sense a meaningful statement about God. I did say that "we live in the time of the death of God" by which I meant that the thread linking heaven and earth, God and man had been broken. What I did not then realize was that while this was an accurate metaphor for the spiritual condition of much of western civilization, it was not and could not be an accurate perception of the spiritual condition of mankind as a whole. I was reacting to the radical denial of ultimate moral or religious norms that characterized western civilization. I was fully aware of the fact that millions of men and women in every western country continued to believe in God and to conduct their lives, insofar as they were able, in accordance with their inherited faith. Although I did not spell out what I meant sociologically, the phenomenon to which I referred was intrinsic to the modernization process as that process had unfolded in the West. I define that process as entailing the progressive rationalization of the economy and society. I understand rationalization, as did Max Weber, as involving "the methodical attainment of a definitely given and practical end by an increasingly precise calculation of adequate mean."[1] To the extent that an economy or a society is fully rationalized in the formal sense, *all* values and institutions that impede the efficient attainment of its practical ends will be rejected, even if these values are hallowed by immemorial custom or religious tradition. As Weber understood, in a fully rationalized economy impersonal calculations of profit and loss would eliminate all considerations based upon shared feelings of fraternity, kinship, community or even simple humanity. Moreover, once set in motion such a system is internally compulsive. Failure to conform to its rules brings in its train the most severe economic penalties. This is especially true of advanced technological societies in which the scale of investment is so large that failure to meet the test of rationality in planning, manufacturing, marketing and distribution can result in catastrophic loss, as the American automobile industry has recently learned to its extreme distress.

When I spoke of our era as "the time of the death of God," I had in mind the social, economic and political consequences of the modernization process as suggested above. I first became interested in the modernization process as a result of my research into the phenomenon of large-scale programs of state-sponsored population elimination such as the destruction of the European Jews, the Armenians, and, more recently, the Cambodians.[2] This is not the occasion to discuss that work in detail, but in all three instances once the decision was taken by the political decision-makers, no religious sentiment or value proved efficacious in halting the program. The personnel involved had only one imperative, the effective fulfillment of one's assigned task. For the vast majority of the functionaries all other considerations of value were effectively eliminated. Furthermore, such behavior was entirely consistent with Weber's description of the normal behavior of bureaucratic functionaries in both modern economic and political institutions.[3] Put differently, such behavior was not a "throwback" to an earlier, more "barbaric" age, as some would suggest, but an expression of the modern spirit itself.[4]

In the face of a culture that proved to be practically Godless, no matter what the private religious sentiments of the individuals who comprised that culture might be, it is altogether understandable that sensitive individuals might turn to traditional religious institutions as a counter to a normless and valueless culture. Indeed the revival of religion in the United States in the past decade has been a reaction to the threat of anomy that a world that is practically Godless inevitably entails. There is obviously a limit to the kind of moral and spiritual anarchy that had begun to characterize the advanced technological societies of the West. Nevertheless, we must ask whether the current revival is likely to provide an adequate long-term response to the problems of relativism, skepticism and normlessness that has afflicted the modern world and that led Dostoevski to depict Ivan Karamazov as asserting, "If there is no God, all things are permitted."

Unfortunately, there are good reasons for believing that *the radical secularism to be found in the West is not a cultural force independent of western religion but an unintended consequence of it.* Permit me to offer an example of what I mean. In the part of the United States in which I live there are huge pine forests that are periodically cut down and replanted by the corporations that own the forests. The behavior of the corporations is an example of the rationalizing spirit of modernity. The trees are simply regarded as a commodity to be produced in accordance with a planned schedule to meet the demands of the world market. There is nothing inherently sacred in the trees. For the corporation and even the local people, trees are there simply to be cut down and used by man. Yet, such an attitude is by no means universal. In many parts of the world trees are thought to be possessed by spirits and hence to be sacred. An important moment in the history of western religion came when the Emperor Charlemagne deliberately caused to be cut down trees in the Saxon forests as a means of demonstrating that the trees were possessed of neither deities nor spirits. Although most people in the West today take it for granted that woods, mountains and streams are simply natural objects devoid of any inherent sacrality, an extraordinary spiritual revolution had to take place before people could so regard the phenomena of the physical world. Moreover, this transformation was part of a larger revolution in which human political institutions were radically desacralized. Where once the majority of mankind believed that an aura of divinity encompassed their rulers and their political institutions, both rulers and governing institutions have normally come to be regarded as purely human institutions.

The cultural process whereby the natural and human world came to be regarded as devoid of any inherent sacrality has been identified as that of *Entzauberung der Welt*, the disenchantment of the world. According to Max Weber, where such disenchantment occurs "there are in principle no mysterious forces that come into play, but rather one can, in principle, master all thing by calculation."[5] Inevitably, such disenchantment leads to radical secularization. Where this process reaches its logical conclusion, the world is regarded as totally godless and hence anomic, a condition that most men and women find intolerable.

It is sometimes claimed that the process of disenchantment and secularization is the result of modern intellectual criticism of traditional beliefs and institutions. In reality, it is highly unlikely that secularism could have taken hold as a mass phenomenon on the basis of intellectual criticism alone. Every person is born into the world in such a way that fear, reverence and awe of sacred institutions, traditions and powers can be inculcated with overwhelmingly powerful emotional force long before he or she acquires the faculty of critical reflection. If, for example, I had been taught from earliest childhood that the trees in my garden are the abode of sacred spirits and that I must be ever on my guard not to injure them, it is not likely that a university course in biology or philosophy could change my mind about the trees. Only a religious faith that is radically polemic to the forces of magic and to belief in the earth's indwelling spirits could have legitimated the profound spiritual, cultural and psychological revolution that was necessary before an entire civilization could reject and negate that which men and women had revered as sacred from time immemorial. Moreover, only one religious tradition proclaimed the existence of an absolutely sovereign Power, upon whom all things without exception were utterly dependent for their existence, who was unremittingly hostile to the powers of magic and polytheism. Given the exclusive power of that sovereign Power, those who accepted him as their God, at least in the West, felt they had no alternative but to assume a posture of radical hostility towards the sacred spirits and traditions of the rest of mankind. In his claim to total and exclusive worship, the transcendent God of Biblical monotheism demanded that his followers regard all other gods, powers and spirits as of no account. Put differently, belief in the God of the Bible involved a radical rejection of any sort of belief in the reality of the spirit world, at least in the West. This attitude is characteristically expressed by the Psalmist:

> "Great is the Lord and worthy of all praise.
> He is more to be feared than all gods.
> For the gods of the nations are idols every one;
> But the Lord made the heavens." (Ps. 96:4-5)

A similar attitude is to be found in Deutero-Isaiah:

> "Thus saith the Lord, King of Israel,
> the Lord of Hosts, his Redeemer:

I am the first and I am the last,
and there is no God but me." (Isaiah 44:6)

If one wants to find the origins of the modern secular world, one
can find its beginnings here. Only those who believed in God's unique
sovereignty could safely abandon belief in magic, spirits and powers
and create a world that was as subject to mankind's absolute mastery
as men were subject to God's mastery. This is evident in the incident of
Charlemagne and the trees. It was only because Charlemagne believed
in the one God of the Bible that he was liberated from fear of the
spirits of the woodland groves and did not hesitate to cut down the
trees. He could not have foreseen that a day would come when men
would lose all reverence for nature and see the forest simply as a
source of monetary gain. Nevertheless, disenchantment of the world,
or radical desacralization and secularization, is the indispensable precondition of the rationalization of the economy and society which is
the fundamental characteristic of modernization and capitalism. Thus,
the *paradoxical precondition of a radically secularizing attitude that has effectively
eliminated all religious values from both the economy and the productive processes of the
modern world was a religious revolution.* A further paradox is that the very
absence of religious values which is characteristic of modern secular
capitalism is an unintended consequence of the cultural triumph of
the polemic attitude to the gods, spirits and traditions of the non-
biblical world. This point of view is, of course, thoroughly consistent
with the insights of Max Weber on the biblical roots of the
disenchantment of the world and the role of Calvinism in the emergence of rational bourgeois capitalism. Crucial to Calvinism's role in
creating the modern world has been the fact that it affirmed with far
greater consistency than ever before the transcendence, exclusiveness
and sovereignty of the biblical God. Unlike Judaism, which was the
religion of a small group of outsiders, Calvinism was the predominant
religious force precisely in those communities in which capitalism
experienced its initial impetus.

If the above analysis has any merit, it would follow that a return
to the traditional biblical faith of the West will not serve as a
long-range antidote for the negative cultural and moral consequences

of contemporary secular civilization. The economic achievements of rational bourgeois capitalism, by which I mean the civilization in which formal rationality has achieved its greatest success, are in a certain sense the unintended consequences of religious values that are rooted in faith in the sovereign and radical transcendence of the unique God of biblical monotheism. But note: these values have had a totally secularizing effect! Faith in the sovereignty of this God has intensified our sense of the worldliness of the world and of the futility of mastering the world other than through methodically organized, disciplined, systematic calculation. Moreover, the theological consequences of the affirmation of the radical transcendence of this God, both by virtue of the utter inaccessibility of his transcendent nature and by virtue of the suspicion that by means of relating to him, even in prayer and religious worship itself, might be a form of magic.[6] In the final analysis, as Weber understood, those who believe in this God have no choice but rationally to pursue their vocations wholly within the world, the one remaining link to their God being their faith that he has manifested his sovereignty by causing them to prosper in their vocations. Worldly success is pursued in early capitalism not for the sake of consumption or any of the superfluous gratifications that affluence might bring, but because it offers the believer, cut off from God by an impossible transcendence, the last remaining hint of whether or not he has been accepted by God.

There are many reasons why Weber remains worthy of study today, not the least is the insight implicit in his work that modernization is Christian in its origins and that, even when it has lost its original religious motivation, it nevertheless represents both an intrinsic and a socio-cultural expression of the triumph of the world view of what he called "ascetic Protestantism." Put differently, the Weber hypothesis implies that modernization represents a highly successful form of Christianization even when it is adopted by non-Christians who continue to be faithful to their ancestral religious traditions. Lest I be misunderstood, I do not offer these observations because of any desire to foster Christianity among non-Christians but because I see no other way to interpret the socio-cultural meaning of the phenomenon of modernization. Here again Weber is instructive. Commenting on the modern world, Weber observed that:

> The fate of our time is characterized by rationalization and, above all, by the 'disenchantment of the world.'

In essence to modernize means to rationalize and to "disenchant," but, as we have seen, it is only with the triumph of Protestant Christianity and its doctrine of the radical and unique sovereignty of the transcendent Creator God that such rationalization becomes possible for whole masses of people rather than for a small group of intellectual elites.

Yet, if modernization is a form of Christianization, there is great irony in the fact, that as a form of secularization, modernization is an expression of self-negating Christianization. This does not mean that Christian Churches have lost their power or their numbers. On the contrary in the United States they are gaining in strength, but do Christian religious values have the power to dethrone morally-neutral economic values where the survival of great financial institutions are at stake? To pose this question in this form is to answer it as did Weber:

> The material development of an economy on the basis of social associations flowing from market relationships generally follows its objective rules, disobedience to which entails economic failure and, in the long run, economic ruin.[8]

Is there then no way out of a civilization of quantifying rationality that has the effect of dissolving all spiritual and ethical values? Are we condemned to the "iron cage" of the future, as Weber suggested, or is there a way out? It is my conviction that the situation is by no means hopeless although no man can predict the outcome. If we are correct that only a religious revolution could have brought about the transformations of consciousness that led to the disenchantment of the world and eventually to modernization, then in all likelihood, it will take a transformation of consciousness originating in religion to overcome the present situation. Unfortunately, genuine religious transformations cannot be brought about simply because their need is deeply felt. Moreover, such transformations must originate with men and women of inspiration, inspiration that is credible. They cannot originate with contemporary western-trained theologians or religious scholars. The theological training received by most clergymen in the West, whether Protestant or Jewish, and to a certain extent Roman Catholic, is an expression of the same spirit of rationality that has brought forth the modern world. It is, for example, impossible to receive a theological degree from any mainstream western institution without studying the basic texts of the biblical religions as if they were literary documents to be investigated in the same spirit of critical inquiry as any other historical document. One might say that the disenchantment process, with its attendant secularization, has expressed itself not only outside of the religious community but also in the way religious professionals are currently trained. This is understood by those Orthodox Jews and Fundamentalist Christians who continue to regard the Bible as literally the word of God. Nevertheless, it is impossible for western religious communities to overcome secularization when the very way they train their professionals is itself an expression of the secularization process. If credible, world-transforming religious inspiration is needed in our times, it is not likely to come from either the scholars or the clergy trained in the modern institutions of the western world. I include myself in this category. This is not because of any flaw in the character of the religious professionals but because of the unavoidably secular nature of the training which is today an indispensable prerequisite of their certification. In spite of themselves, they are fully a part of the rational spirit of the age. This is part of what I meant when I said that we live in the time of the "death of God."

It is, however, my conviction that possibilities for spiritual renewal exist in the Orient which may have an important long-range impact on the world as a whole. Lest I be misunderstood, I do not see the conventional American experiments in oriental religion or fundamentalism as the way out of the "iron cage." The fundamentalist renaissance represents a return to biblical religion, but if, as we have argued, modern secular culture is an unintended consequence of the triumph of biblical religion, then any return to biblical religion, unless it is combined with some new spiritual element, can only have the long-range effect of further intensifying the rationality of the modernization process.

Although it is too early to offer a judgment on whether the Unification Church will be the effective agent of the spiritual renewal that is required if we are to find a way out of the "iron cage," it does offer certain elements of promise. The rest of this paper is devoted to a brief enumeration of some of these elements:

Charismatic Leadership. If it is the fate of the biblical religions to negate themselves in ever-widening areas of human endeavor, only a religious leader who can with credibility claim the authority to define what is to be permitted and what prohibited is likely to overcome the value-free character of the present situation. While such value-definition is possible today on the part of religious authorities, it is largely limited to matters of private morality. It has little effect on the larger community. Neither mainstream Jewish nor Protestant clergymen have effective value-defining authority. They are largely salaried professionals who know their social location and its constraints. Charismatic leadership can be derived either from the office or the person of the leader. As we know, the papacy is an institution whose authority derives from office charisma. The leader of the Unification Church derives his authority from personal charisma.

His claim to authority is based upon his experience of having been commissioned to carry on and perhaps to complete the work of redemption commenced by other great religious figures of the past. Moreover, his claim carries with it what can minimally be described as a psychological authority that no western religious figure could possibly possess. He comes from a country in which indigenous shamanistic religion co-exists with Protestant Christianity in a way that would be utterly impossible in the West. According to the English scholar Spencer J. Palmer, the revival of indigenous Korean religion was an important element in fostering the spread of Christianity in that country. Palmer maintains that Koreans were able to identify Hananim, the High God of their indigenous tradition, with the biblical God.

Palmer also holds that the traditions that assert that (a) Hananim gave life to the people by sending his divine son into the world and (b) that Hananim's grandson Tan'gun was the first Korean king seemed to many Koreans closer to Christianity than to either Buddhism or Confucianism.[9] If Palmer is correct, Korean Christianity was in general never as hostile to or removed from the nation's original spiritual traditions as was the case in most predominantly Protestant countries. Hence the turning of the Korean people to Christianity was less uprooting and less alienating than elsewhere. Put differently, Korean Christians, or at least a goodly number of them, did not experience the kind of "disenchantment of the world" that was experienced in the West. It has therefore been possible for religiously-inspired Koreans to claim to have received communications from the spirit world with none of the self-doubt or imputation of bad faith that would inevitably attend such assertions were they made by a western religious leader. Of course, it is possible to reduce the Rev. Moon's experiences to the categories of western psychology of religion, but to do so is merely to translate the terminology used in one culture to describe a phenomenon to that used in another. There is absolutely no reason for asserting that one mode of description is superior to another. Insofar as the Rev. Moon is not cut off from the sources of inspiration present in indigenous Korean religious culture, he may be able to infuse his movement with a spirit of inspiration that is no longer possible in the secularizing and disenchanted West. That he has been able to inspire an impressive number of persons both in the East and the West is evident from the growth of the Church.

Obviously, charismatic leadership has a certain element of instability in it as Weber understood. It serves best an as agent of radical change. Its long-range effects can only be ascertained over time, perhaps only after the charisma has been routinized. Yet, it is interesting to note that at least one important German historian of sociology, Wolfgang Mommsen, has claimed that Weber came to see charismatic leadership as the only hope of overcoming the "iron cage" of a bureaucratically-ossified modern world. Because of the horrendous experience with charismatic leadership experienced by Germans during the period of National Socialism, there has understandably been much controversy over Mommsen's attempt to depict Weber as in any sense favoring what could be regarded as the *Führerprinzip.* Yet, Mommsen's observations cannot be easily dismissed. In a structured world in which each person is required to fulfill his assigned task without concerning himself with the value of what he does, somebody must decide in the area of values. According to Mommsen, Weber came to the conclusion that the charismatic leader would ultimately be that person.[10]

I find no reason seriously to question Mommsen's basic conclusions, while fully recognizing the hazards involved in charismatic leadership. There is, however, one fundamental difference between Weber's charismatic value-creator and religious charismatic leaders such as the Rev. Sun Myung Moon. Weber's charismatic leader is the great man who is responsible to no one save himself. Moon's charisma is based upon a claim of divine commission that places him in a line of religious leaders and thus is likely to have certain safeguards that a leader responsible only to himself would lack. Obviously, the Rev. James Jones can be offered as proof that the safeguards are a slender thread on which to rely, but Jones and his community were involved in a strategy of separation and withdrawal from the world whereas the Unification Church is thoroughly engaged in the world it hopes to transform.

I should like to conclude this section with a comment that is both personal and theological. When I participated in the so-called death-of-God movement, I was in a sense saying that the theological enterprise could go no further. Moreover, I was acutely conscious of the fact that I and my peers were the generation after Tillich. I was convinced then and remain convinced today that no purely intellectual enterprise in the domain of theology could transcend the "death of God." I also knew that were some religious figure to present himself as divinely commissioned, a fundamentally new element would be introduced into the contemporary religious situation that would transcend the "death of God." Theologians can *reflect* on those who claim to have been commissioned by God. They do not claim such a commission. My attitude to the Rev. Sun Myung Moon is one of respectful and sympathetic appreciation of what he has achieved and promises to achieve in the future. I have until now found no way in which I can evaluate his claims. Were I to do so by customary method, that is the interpretation of religion in terms of the psychology and sociology of religion, I would merely be incorporating his experience into my system without having come any closer to an accurate evaluation of it. Of one thing I am convinced. Only a charismatic religious figure could extricate us from the "iron cage" of secularity and modernity. I will concede that the Rev. Moon is the most significant charismatic leader to arise in our times.

   The Millenarian Character of the Unification Church. Millenarian movements arise at moments of great historical crisis when the customary institutions and traditions are no longer adequate as cultural and/or spiritual vehicles for coping with the situations in which large numbers of people find themselves. As is well known, the dislocations that have attended modernization frequently result in the rise of millenarian movements. This was the case with the Cargo cults of the Pacific Islands as well as the millenarian movements that have arisen in Japan and elsewhere in the orient in the twentieth century. That the present time is one of historical crisis would seem to be obvious. Moreover, there is one respect in which the crisis has deepened spiritually as contrasted with the pre-World War II period. In that period the substitute ideologies of right and left-wing politics still seemed credible as alternatives to a religion that had failed of credibility at least among the intellectuals. Today, both fascism and communism still have their adherents, but the historical failure of both the regimes of the right and the left, such as Nazi Germany and communist Russia, render the political alternatives less attractive as surrogate faiths than they once were. Yet, the need for spiritual and cultural transformation remains. It has been said that millenarian movements can be pre- and post-political. Yet, such movements have been known to act as agents of both religious and social transformation. There is risk in the fact that the Unification Church is a millenarian movement as there is risk in the fact that it is led by a charismatic figure. Yet, it is precisely in these elements of risk that the movement may also find its ability to be a genuine agent of transformation.

 The Asian Origin of the Church. As one who believes that, both economically and politically, the center of gravity of world civilization is in the process of shifting from the Atlantic to the Pacific, I find the Asian origins of the Unification Church a distinct advantage to it. At one level, the Unification Church has almost single-handedly, reversed the historic role of the Christian missions. Until its advent, Christian missionary efforts were almost exclusively those undertaken by western churches to effect the spiritual transformation of the non-western parts of the world. The Unification Church is the first church of purely Asian origin to carry its mission successfully to the West. Moreover, it has done so with a degree of intelligence, sophistication and style that is perhaps unparalleled in the history of Christian missionary efforts in modern times. One result of the Church's mission has been the fact that a number of western thinkers, among whom I include myself, have been exposed to Asia and Asian religion in a direct and immediate way that would not have been possible otherwise. We have yet to be able to calculate the extent to which the Unification Church has come at precisely the moment when the balance between East and West had shifted decisively. Perhaps the moment at which western religion had come to the dead end of the "iron cage" was followed by the kind of shift from one civilization to another that makes a new beginning possible. In human history, every new era has witnessed its own characteristic spiritual response. It is doubtful that many moments in human history have been as laden with the potentialities for new material and spiritual beginnings as the inauguration of the Pacific era. With that new beginning the Unification Church has a unique and unparalleled opportunity. Hopefully, it will grasp that opportunity. Hopefully, it will give to humanity a new fulfillment for a very old idea: Ex Oriente Lux, Light out of The East.

FOOTNOTES

[1]Max Weber, "The Sociology of the World Religions," in H. H. Gerth and C. Wright Mills, eds., *From Max Weber: Essays in Sociology* (New York: Oxford Univ. Press, 1946), p.293.

[2]See Richard L. Rubenstein, *The Cunning of History* (New York: Harper & Row, 1975).

[3]See Weber, "Bureaucracy," in Gerth and Mills, pp. 215 ff.

[4]See Rubenstein, pp. 78 ff.

[5]See Weber, "Science As A Vocation" in Gerth and Mills, p. 293.

[6]See Peter Berger, *The Sacred Canopy* (New York: Doubleday, 1966), pp. 111 ff.

[7]Weber, "Science As A Vocation," p. 155.

[8]Max Weber, *Economy and Society: An Outline of Interpretive Sociology* (New York: Bedminster, 1968), 2, 636ff.

[9]See Spencer J. Palmer, *Korea and Christianity: The Problem of Identification With Tradition* (Seoul: Hollym, 1967), pp. 5-18.

[10]See Wolfgang J. Mommsen, *The Age of Bureaucracy: Perspectives on the Political Sociology of Max Weber* (Oxford: Basil Blackwell, 1974). For a discussion of the Mommsen thesis, see Raymond Aron, "Max Weber and Power-Politics," in Otto Stammer, *Max Weber and Sociology Today* (New York: Harper & Row, 1971), pp. 83-100; and the responses to Aron by Carl J. Friedrich, Hans Paul Bahrdt, Wolfgang J. Mommsen, Karl W. Deutsch, Eduard Baumgarten and Adolf Arnt.

The God of Principle:
A Critical Evaluation

Frederick Sontag

I.

The average person, whether layman or theologian, approaches the Unification Church with newspaper and magazine headlines ringing in his or her ears. Given the sensationalism surrounding the rapid expansion of the followers of Sun Myung Moon from the mid-1960s to mid-1970s and the controversy which surrounded this, it could hardly be otherwise. However, our task is not to evaluate the barrage of media criticism, nor to evaluate the program and practices of the Unification movement, but to understand and appraise the view of the nature of God which lies behind it. This is a proper theological task. And the theme of this essay will be that their view of the Principle according to which God acts is both Rev. Moon's 'revelation' and the key to understanding the actions of the Holy Spirit Association for the Unification of World Christianity (the movement's original name), as well as its attractiveness to young people worldwide. The general public hears about street fundraising in America, real estate purchases and business ventures, but these activities attract few to be disciples of Rev. Moon. The rare insight he offers into God's plan to create a new world, however, does.

The Mission of Jesus is, of course, also central, as well as Moon's account of the Fall and the entrance of evil into human nature. But these are secondary, derivative doctrines, which depend on his initial insight into the Principle according to which God acts. Even members are not in full agreement about what 'Principle' means, although it is central to the thought and life of each convert. The outside public quite naturally believes that the devotion of each disciple is to Rev. and Mrs. Moon as persons, as True Parents.

Their place is central in the concept of the new unified Family and the arranged, blessed marriages which are to inaugurate the God-centered families that Adam and Eve, and Jesus too, failed to start. Although the relationship of Moon to the Principle is both complex and subtle, his place is determined more by the concept of the Principle of God's action rather than vice versa. The key to conversion of new disciples is their acceptance of the teaching of the Principle, which itself is not quite identical with the book now entitled Divine Principle,[1] just as the Word of God may be revealed in the Bible without being identical to the printed word of a certain version of that scripture.

The core of the subtlety, of course, is that the revelation, and the development of the Principle, came to and through Rev. Moon in his early years in Korea. In traditional fashion, he preached the Principle orally before it was written down, and the earlier written versions were less elaborately filled out with historical accounts than the present standard text. Some of the added material came from sources other than Moon, and the book can be revised (he says he will do so) without damage to the core of the Principle. The members speak of it as the Completed Testament, since the key to God's intended action is the revelation of this Principle which was reserved to be made clear in these latter days. God has not rejected the program of the Old or New Testament, but, as some scripture indicates, he did not reveal every detail of his projected action or time table at first. He reserved some disclosures for a later day when the Kingdom of Heaven on Earth would be inaugurated. Just as the early Christian Church viewed Old Testament scripture as preparation for the New, so Moonists look on the New Testament as a preparation for God's action in the last days, now outlined by the communication of the Principle via Rev. Moon.

One key to this new understanding of God's revealed way of action involves the use of "central figures" as God's instrument for affecting the course of human events. Adam, Moses, Abraham, Jesus were such central figures, and now Moon is called to that crucial position in a pivotal time. The question of whether Moon is a new messiah, or the Lord of the Second Advent predicted by the Principle, is not so important and is subject to a variety of affirmations. But it is hard to conceive of anyone following Moon, or putting up with the demanding and sacrificial life involved, unless he or she believed Moon to be the central figure selected by God as his instrument in the present age. As we shall see, such election does not necessarily mean success for the mission, but Principle teaches that the primary meaning of faith is the identification of such a central figure or figures and uniting with them to try again to institute God's Kingdom on earth, God's goal since creation. Lack of unity with the central figure, which means a lack of centering love in God's purpose, is the primary reason for previous failures in God's program, and thus it is the chief sin in the spiritual world of Rev. Moon.

II.

So much by way of setting the scene for describing God and his principle of action. Let us proceed first to scan *Divine Principle* for its description of God's plan of action, next summarize this, and then offer an evaluation. I say "God's plan of action" rather than "God's nature" since *Divine Principle* offers an activist, pragmatic account. To be sure, God's nature is outlined in a metaphysical description of his attributes, but God is primarily to be understood, and related to, according to our understanding of his principle of action. I know no member who is devoted to the account of the elements of God's nature, but many who are convinced that they now understand 'God's heart,' the principle of his action, and the plan according to which he would now have them act and serve him. In a day in which God has been pronounced dead by theologians and placed in limbo by skepticism, underneath the sensationalism the most important fact about the rise of the Unified Family (a name they once used for themselves) is the strength of the individual member's assurance that, at last, he understands God's plan. This is now available to him thanks to Rev. Moon's suffering (paying of indemnity) to overcome Satanic forces and uncover the Principle.

The key to understanding and appraising the Unification view of God, I will argue, lies with this account of God's newly revealed principle of action. If you understand and accept the Principle, and Moon as its instrument, you are a Moonist. However, the metaphysical-theological issue underlying this is: (1) Whether God is bound to the detail of the Principle, or whether he remains independent from it and could revise it; and (2) Whether he did save the climax of his progressive revelation until this latter day and choose a new nation (Korea) for its expression. Also, even if all this is accepted, has God's revelation now closed with the expression of the Principle, or could God act again at some future time to alter his program? This, of course, reduces to the question of whether, even if one accepted this later revelation and the disclosure of God's principle of action, God is identical with this revelation or is independent of it. Many who reject the Unification Church do so because they take revelation to be closed at some time in the past and thus no longer open. For Moonists, the issue is whether revelation is still open after the Principle.

Setting aside the fundamental issue of whether God could alter a past revelation and open yet another new future, what is the Unification view of God's nature and the Principle of his action? As confirmation of this way of approach to the Unification view of the nature of God, note that the church's chief theologian, Young Oon Kim, has no section in her book, Unification Theology and Christian Thought[2], specifically on God. There is a chapter on Christology and the Mission of Jesus, but the rest of the work outlines God's action and his plan for the future in the Principle of Creation, the Fall of Man, the History of Restoration, etc. Of course, God lurks about on every page. Moonists are ever-sensitive to God's aims versus some Christian groups which center on the sacraments, on liturgy, or on social programs. Thus, Professor Kim is always describing God, not so much directly or metaphysically but in terms of his program, human history, and the future. Rev. Moon uses metaphysical concepts to describe God in Divine Principle but I see no attachment on his part to the unalterable truth of these concepts. They seem symbolic or suggestive, and thus alterable. It is the core of the Principle of God's action in history that is normative.

From the devoutness of the core members of the Movement and its worldwide spread, we know it is possible to relate to God on the basis of the Principle and experience a sense of the presence of the divine. To me this does not indicate that it is the sole avenue to God, nor even the preferable one, but it does tell us that it is one of the ways men and women can be brought to see God, sometimes with considerable impact. Since *Divine Principle* begins with the Principle of Creation, we know that this is the beginning of its approach to God. True, Genesis is the first book in the Bible as we have the canon, and it begins with the creation story. However, since Unification theology is a variant of Christianity, it is important to note that the New Testament writers sometimes take a different approach. True, the office and mission of Jesus have often been interpreted in terms of Old Testament expectations, and some Christian groups still rely heavily on Old Testament sources and images. Nevertheless, it would be difficult to say that Genesis forms the context of traditional Christian teaching in the same way that it does for the Unification view of God.

In other words, Jesus' mission as the Christ is understood in terms of a more general outline of God's action in creation and history, rather than Jesus himself serving as the center. This is neither unique nor necessarily bad, but it is true that Moonists speak more about God and less about Jesus. Or more accurately, they relate directly to God and understand Jesus within their new view of God, rather than God's sole self-revelation being found in Jesus. Mediation to God is via the Principle and its disclosures, in which to be sure Jesus plays a central role, but not as the sole incarnation of God. To go further on this theme would take us into Unification Christology, but it is important to go at least this far in order to understand how God is approached and what this tells us about both the divine nature and Jesus' office. Since Jesus offered a central revelation, but not the only revelation of God, and since revelation was not closed but remains open, to understand God it is necessary to search out the movement of the Holy Spirit in the present age. Then, we use this new insight as the key to piece together God's past actions with his future intentions—which is what Rev. Moon did in his prayer and biblical study to uncover the Principle.

III.

Divine Principle opens by suggesting that we all seek happiness, which is attained when our desires are fulfilled. We can go the path of unrighteousness, but we each have an "original mind" (p. 9) which seeks happiness by delight in the law of God. Through the fall, we have lost our ability to follow the original mind and so are caught in great contradictions. At this point Moon makes his first assumption about God, that he would not have created man with such a contradiction (divided nature) (p. 3,). This rationalist assumption is so basic to Unification views of God that it is hard to over stress the importance of its consequences. It sets the Moonist in opposition to the Existentialist, for example. As we will see, it is the beginning of a series of restrictions Divine Principle places on God which have the paradoxical consequence of both revealing a clear pattern of God's activity for the believer to relate to while at the same time binding God rigidly to that schedule. For instance, the Introduction already sounds the important theme of the necessity to unify science and religion (p. 4), so that the church's cultural endeavors (e.g., dance and musical groups, conferences) become central to God's program, but it also binds his success to the outcome of questionable projects (e.g., bringing cultures together, uniting science and religion).

It may be that no one can have a revelation of God that is concrete without binding God to the detail of the form of the revelation. Still, it is possible to see God and announce that vision but add that this may not be the only way in which God either can appear or may choose to do so. Although Moonists believe in a contingency in God's program, so that he does not relate to the world as a necessary process the precise details of which he foreknows, there is fixity in the Moonist assurance that theirs is indeed the program of action God will adhere to. Perhaps involved in the very notion of receiving a revelation, whether it be Moon or Luther, is the overwhelming conviction that this is the conclusive insight into divinity. However, it is possible to coordinate this with a sense of the divine mystery, the hidden though revealed God, so that one's increased learning about divinity is a "learned ignorance" as Cusanus puts it. One learns, sees, penetrates, feels God revealed but at the same time sees larger mysteries opened which the spiritual novice cannot be aware of. At the moment, followers of the Principle seem inflexible in their certainty of God's ways, but perhaps this is typical of the fresh convert's attitude and not so true of Moon himself. The disciple's test in relation to God will come if he ignores the script or alters his prescribed lines. At that point they will need to decide whether they were wrong in their first perception, or whether God keeps an escape clause in all his contracts. (If I were God dealing with man, I would.)

Like most new revelations, *Divine Principle* comes at a time when it sees Christianity in confusion and ineffective (p. 7). As with Luther, Kierkegaard, Augustine, or George Fox, a decline in spirituality and the loss of institutional vigor seem to provide an occasion for fresh revelation. Some movements press for a new strict spirituality in their disgust with the world. The Principle asserts that the worlds of spirit and flesh must be "joined in perfect unity" (p. 8). This makes it opt for a heaven realized on earth (c.f. Marxism) and promote an activism in the world to bring about God's plan. Physical happiness is important, since the physical body is not an obstacle but a means to achieve spiritual perfection in harmony. Divine Principle evidences its origins in a time of high optimism over the fruits of the physical sciences when it insists that the road to unity requires interpreting things "scientifically" (p. 8). This assumes the singularity and finality of scientific theory as if it were one thing, a hope many shared in the first half of this century but few do today. God, then, is scientific in his procedure.

The whole vision is one of science approaching religion and religion approaching science. They only wait for "a new expression of truth" (p. 9) to bring these diverse realms together in a final consummation. Again the question is not so much whether our perception of science has changed since the first half of the century or even whether religion can be interpreted scientifically, as many others hoped also, as whether God achieves his purpose by these movements within culture. If he did, it would be easier, but the problem is that God is then bound to a cultural project and thus subject to defeat if that project fails or changes. However, the new truth which can accomplish this unity "should enable us to know God as reality" (p. 10). Thus, the conviction, and the assumption, is that God stands at last fully revealed—at least to the vanguard of this new truth (c.f. Marxism) if not yet to all. The question, then, is whether any such final knowledge of God is possible in the nature of the case, given God and given human capacities. The question is also whether God chooses to work in this way of progressive and then, at last, final revelation of his principle. Surely to feel oneself in possession of that principle, now fully revealed, is an overpowering experience.

We have sought unity among religions for some time, and Unification thought sees this as God's way. There should be a truth which can unite all existing religions in one absolute way (p. 11). This project involves enormous assumptions about the nature of religions (e.g., that they are such as to be able to be unified on any basis) and about God (e.g., that he moves by uniting all religions), both of which involve serious questions. Is it the case that God desires all men to live together in brotherly love under God as our Parent on this earth (p. 12)? The key to accomplish this is, of course, the liquidation of sin. Again like Marx, Moon thinks he has located evil in a single source and possesses the formula for its eradication (with God's help, of course). God has been manipulating history toward this end, which brings in the major assumption: that God works by and through the processes of history. This, too, like the confidence in science and the ideal of unifying all religions, is a child of the nineteenth century, so that perhaps the crucial issue concerning God is whether he does in fact use history in this way. But God has sent a messenger to resolve the fundamental questions of life and the universe: Sun Myung Moon.

Are the heavenly secrets now brought to light by one who has fought against Satanic forces in the spiritual and physical world and won a victory (p. 16)? Again, we have the question of whether God operates in such a fashion, or whether his secrets are revealed more as a surprise gift than as a reward for conquests. Chapter one of *Divine Principle* is the "Principle of Creation." This is the focal point where the ones who come after the spiritual revealer begin their search to understand God too. Until this day no one has known the plan for the creation of man (p. 19), so that 'Principle' primarily means: the final coming to light of this plan as the result of the struggle of the central figure in our age. The assumption is that we know God's characteristics by observing the created world. This question has long been argued by philosophers. But *Divine Principle* is not really a natural theology, since even after Rev. Moon's spiritual and physical struggle and God's decision to reveal his plan in our time, the 'average man' cannot discern God's nature simply by empirical observation. He must study Principle intently and devoutly, and he must struggle spiritually and physically ("pioneer") at the same time.

IV.

At this point a metaphysical principle is introduced, which governs not only God and his creation but the activity of all men, particularly those whose lives try to embody the Principle. A creation cannot come into being, we are told "unless a reciprocal relationship between positivity and negativity has been achieved" (p. 20). Male and female are treated as having essentially the dual characteristics of positivity and negativity. It is not clear whether this way of proceeding is binding or is only one expression for how God creates. Also there is the even more central notion of 'external form' and 'internal character' (p. 21). This makes it evident that God's nature is not governed by unity first of all, rather, a balance of dual characteristics is primary. External form is the visible counterpart of the internal character, and subjective and objective position govern these relationships. God exists as absolute subject, "having characteristics of both essential character and essential form" (p. 24). God's existence is governed by a reciprocal relationship between the dual characteristics of internal and external, and also masculinity and femininity.

The Universe is God's substantial object, and *Divine Principle* then quotes the I Ching in support of its notion of God's dual characteristics. However, the traditional Western metaphysical notion of God's self-existent nature is affirmed. "Give and take" is a way of process, and the universe is seen as forming give and take action due to the Universal Prime Energy of God (p. 28). Each individual stands as God's object and receives the power necessary for its existence. Thus, 'power' and 'process' are prime concepts for interpreting God, more so than, say, 'substance' or 'being' in traditional theories. Unification views of the nature of God have been compared with Process Theology, and the similarities come out most clearly at this point. However, the Fall cut off man's give and take relationship with God, which indicates Divine Principle's stress on the fall and sin, neither of which are prominent in Process Theology. But fallen man can unite with Jesus in a give and take relationship and be restored to his original nature (p. 30). At this point we see the novelty of the Principle, for it is said to be within man's scope to take the action necessary to restore himself.

The "four position foundation" (p. 32) outlines the intricacies of God's operation and is used in preference to a traditional notion of trinity. God, husband and wife and their offspring manifest the four position foundation, which indicates the centrality of the family in the Unification view of both God and salvation. If the mind centers on God, the body then unites with the mind as the mind becomes one with God, and the individual becomes the substantial object of God. The purpose of creation is restored when man lives centered on God. This would have been accomplished in Adam and Eve had they not fallen. The universe lost its center when man fell.

One might justifiably stop at this point and spend some time analyzing the details of Divine Principle's somewhat novel notion of how God's nature operates. It represents the metaphysical core, and it explains their belief in salvation-through-the-family. The concentration is on male-female unity, which leads to the notion that Jesus' aim was to marry and found the God-centered family which Adam failed to do. However, I believe the core of their faith lies in the overall outline of God's operation, so that this metaphysical account is accepted if the larger picture is accepted, not vice versa.

When it comes to God's relation to creation and his power, the Divine Principle is quite traditional. They can affirm with Haydn in The Creation, "A new created world springs forth at God's command."

Some modern views have abandoned God's absolute control on creation, either limiting him to a role in the process or accepting an evolutionary scheme of progressive creation. However, the mystery in the Principle appears at this point, and I do not believe it is ever dispelled: If God has such absolute power over creation, why is he then bound to observe a certain process in order to accomplish his purposes, rather than exercising his power and restructuring the whole of creation at his will? Furthermore, theodicy is never really explained. That is, did God know Eve would succumb to Satan, and could this have been prevented? Do we live in the only possible order God might have created, or could he have created an order more conducive to our success than the one in which we live? The *Divine Principle* skips over these issues and seems to assume we live in the only order God could have ordained and that it is the best one. But to assume this imposes a questionable restriction on God's creative powers.

Again in accord with part of the Christian tradition, Moon asserts that the purpose of the creation of the universe, and man's coming into existence, is to return joy to God (p. 41). God feels joy as man does when he feels his original character and form objectively through the stimulation derived from his substantial object. The man whose mind and body have formed a four position foundation centered on God becomes God's temple. "This means that man attains deity" (p. 43). Thus, God is very human in conception. He feels joy and suffering, and he achieves joy as man does. But on the other hand, man is not so far from divinity. A man who becomes such an object for the joy of God can never fall, but Adam did not reach this level of human perfection. He needed to go through a process of perfection first, and he and Eve never completed this growth stage. The nature of God's love is expressed in parental love, the conjugal love of husband and wife, and in children's love. This gives us a clue as to why the establishment of perfected families lies at the center of Unification practice, and why the mass marriage ceremony is their primary and only sacrament. When the subject and object center in Satan we have 'evil.' When they center in God we have 'good.' But man fell before he could accomplish the three stages of growth. The Moonist mass marriage 'blessing' begins the process of growth toward perfection again.

When *Divine Principle* says that each being grows autonomously by the power of the Divine Principle and each person has his "own portion of responsibility" (p. 83), we recognize the stress the Principle puts on freedom. God will not interfere and compromise human freedom, and thus his purpose depends on man's responsibility for its fulfillment. There is a program for the restoration of humanity too, and man must follow this in order to restore his dominion over all things. It is by achieving perfect oneness with God's heart that man attains dominion over things, as Adam should have done. Man is the mediator and center of harmony between the two worlds, the invisible substantial world and the visible substantial world. This mediating role has often been reserved for Jesus as the Word in traditional theologies, and *Divine Principle* does say that Jesus came as a perfected man in flesh and spirit in order to perfect fallen men by striving to have them unite with him. The failure of Jesus to obtain this perfect union, and his decision to settle for spiritual perfection, thereby leaving physical perfection and union for another time, is the story of Unification Christology. However, where God's nature is concerned our question is whether the procedure as outlined was and is God's only alternative.

The realization of the Kingdom of Heaven waits on the realization of the Kingdom of God on earth (p. 62), which points out the importance of physical perfection as a base for spiritual perfection. God embodies his own nature in creation and then seems dependent on physical conformity to achieve a spiritual goal. Physical arrangements take on great importance and certainly are not to be disparaged, which explains why Moonists buy neglected real estate and work to restore it. The way to the Kingdom of God is through physical creation and its perfection, not away from it. Since Adam fell, a man must come again who will draw all men to him in harmonious oneness in order to fulfill the ideal of creation (p. 68). It is as if God elected one plan and has no choice but to keep trying until he can make the original plan work. God embodies the process, but he is also bound to it. He used a formula in creating man, and now he must labor through creation until he can find a way to induce men to live up to it. The whole history of Providence is the story of God trying again and again to make the formula work. He controlled creation with full power in his initial act, but paradoxically, he now seems bound by his own hard work.

V.

A slightly different note is introduced when *Divine Principle* asserts: "man was created to live in accordance with the Principle" (p. 80). The notion of returning joy to God is traditional, but now we learn that the lately revealed Principle is the key to all man's understanding. Deviation from the Principle caused the Fall, and living in accord with it starts the process of restoration (salvation) and growth (perfection). Thus, not only could man and history not be fully understood until we became aware of the Principle, but, more important, God could not be fully understood. From the divine perspective, however, the critical issue is whether God adopted this one Principle from a variety of possible ways of procedure, and if so, is he now bound to follow it without recourse to other modes of action? If he is tied to this elaborate plan, a "new Legalism" is introduced, since both God and man are bound to a rigid code of behavior, and the well-being of both depends upon their ability to carry out the formula within history. Neither man nor God has any guarantee of eventual success, although the *Divine Principle* portrait of God presents him as constantly calculating and trying again. He never settles for failure, but he is never assured of success.

Followers of the Principle show a totally serious commitment to carry out the project, and they respond as if the future of the world rested on their shoulders—which it does if *Divine Principle* is correct. Exhaustion and disillusion over making the formula work are the major reasons why some long-time members eventually leave. The project of restoring the world is an all-consuming affair, and the round of practical activity the church engages in is simply the physical counterpart of an equally exhausting spiritual struggle demanded of each full-time member. God is suffering, as he has been for two thousand years or more. He depends for his release on human cooperation, a theme Katzantzakis sounds in *The Saviors of God*. Although many Catholic and Protestant movements are equally austere, the sense of joy and release which characterize some Christian experience of God is largely missing. True, in their singing and witnessing, Moonies smile a lot and convey enthusiasm. But that is largely the result of the exhilaration of feeling that you have at last found God's formula, know the way to perfection, and have begun the uphill battle. It is not, and cannot be for them, the joy of release.

The Principle is nothing else but the power of love (p. 81), we are told. But there are forces which oppose it, the same that made man fall, and so the struggle is intense. Illicit love caused man to deviate from the Principle, so that control of love relationships is a primary matter of concern. It accounts for the Moonist practice of an initial period of celibacy followed by arranged marriages. The trick is to begin the right process and go through the requisite stages of growth, which Adam and Eve did not have a chance to do. Then, after reaching perfection and becoming husband and wife, one enters into God's dominion through absolute love and can no longer fall. Man became Satan's child and formed the four position foundation centered on Satan. The key formula which the Principle brings to us is how to pass through the stages of growth properly, marry, form a four position foundation centered on God, restore creation, and then remain immune to all further sin. From God's perspective, the question about this is: Will it result in perfection? Is the Principle in fact the sole cure for sin, and is God bound to operate in this way only? Could sin arise in other ways from other sources?

The attraction of the way of the Principle, as revealing the secret of God's plan, is powerful. More than one ex-member has left the church through forced deprogramming, or due to some practical disillusionment, but still has maintained that he or she "believes the Principle." Most who are outside the movement do not realize that the initial conversion of new followers takes place by continued study of the Principle through repeated lectures that go into greater and greater detail. Members study the Principle continually or go through refresher courses. The preaching and personal effort of Rev. Moon has little to do with proselytizing, and many members have never seen or met him. The primary confrontation takes place between the individual and the Principle, and converts will compare notes on whether it was the second or third or some other lecture which was the turning point for them in their conversion. Of course, the personal attraction of the members whom the novice meets, or the lecturer (it was never Rev. Moon after the early days in Korea), has a great deal to do with conversion as is true in all religious movements, just as disappointing personal relationships have much to do with members leaving. Still, the Principle as the path to God always forms the core of their religious experience.

The exhilaration that sweeps over the new convert is "we can do it!" Now, with the Principle in hand, man can make Satan come to a natural surrender through accomplishing his "portion of responsibility by his own volition" (p. 85). That is exciting news, to be able to restore perfection, relieve God's suffering, bring God joy, and set mankind on the way to perfection. God will never restore men by force, *Divine Principle* is sure; we must do it. This places it close to the Social Gospel of Rauschenbusch. The Kingdom of God will be realized on earth. The world of evil will be restored to perfect goodness centered on Christ. All this becomes possible now, although it was not before, because we did not possess the Principle to unlock God's plan of action so that we could carry it out. Part has been known and disclosed earlier. Now we can know in full. It is an amazing and awesome responsibility to be part of God's vanguard who carry the plan for human restoration (*c.f.* Marxism again). But from God's perspective we must ask: Even if it is a plan that works for some, is God limited by the Principle, or can he also act outside this new Law?

Divine Principle tells us "there is no freedom apart from the Principle" (p. 91). This is easy to understand where human nature is concerned, since the Principle sees itself as the avenue for release from sin. The question is whether this is also true for God. If men do not live up to their role, even granting it as a correct formula to eliminate sin, can God get free of the path of the Principle and act outside it? Man fell because "the power of non-principled love was stronger than the directive power of the freedom of the original mind" (p. 93). Supposedly the revelation of the Principle gives us the formula to avoid such loss of freedom (the Fall) in the future. The question about the Principle is whether in fact its growth formula and plan of marriage can create God-centered families in which the superior power of non-principled love is at last brought under control, as it has not been since Adam's fall. The question for God is whether his sole plan is to release the formula of the Principle and then allow men to make their way back to perfection after centuries of living in sin.

VI.

We can understand the God-of-Principle's relation to contingency when we consider the account of the Fall. We are told that God "foresaw the possibility of the fallen act" (p. 95) but did not intervene to prevent it, although he is a traditional God with the power to do so. The reasons for God's restraint, which has been left unsolved until the Principle are: 1) Man must perfect himself by accomplishing his portion of responsibility; (2) "God intervenes with beings or acts only within the Principle" (p. 96); and, (3) Man must perfect himself through a course in the Principle before he can dominate all creation, as originally intended. A great deal comes to focus in this account, because we learn that: (1) Man can perfect himself by following the outline of Principle, so that his is essentially a self-salvation, although guided by God and surely impossible without God's final revelation of Principle. (2) God so prizes Principle that he will see man fall before intervening in the course set out for human perfection, which means that God foresees contingencies and not a fixed course of events. But, most important, (3) it is explicitly stated that God will not act outside Principle. Thus, he is a God bound by law.

We also know that God moves only by human instrumentality and never directly. His vessels are fallible; thus his purpose is never sure of completion. Nor can God act directly. He must work through history and peoples and cultures to prepare for the mission of the man he elects. But today we are in the Last Days, which is why the full Principle has finally been revealed. Although Jesus accomplished a high office and managed one half, i.e., spiritual salvation, God holds to no one human instrument but may work through many. We have been hidden from God before, but now, in the Last Days, we may come freely before him (p. 121). A kind of evolution in human nature and culture is realizing its peak. A worldwide culture is developing, centered on Christianity, Divine Principle claims. We must find our True Parents and become children of goodness through rebirth. God moves to restore heavenly sovereignty by degrees, it is asserted (p. 124), which raises the question of whether God does in fact move by slow evolution or by intervention.

At this point Divine Principle shows itself to be a child of nineteenth-century evolutionary optimism, as well as trust in science and the upward rise in culture. Do twentieth-century events support such optimism or give any evidence that God works through culture? However, where God himself is concerned, the question is whether he is bound to such historical work or holds himself more aloof from the workings of cultures. Where man is concerned, the question is whether he too follows an evolutionary cycle on the spiritual level. And the factual question is whether he has in fact, in these last days, "restored his spiritual light" (p. 128). Certainly few now share such optimism about man, given his recent record of performance. But Rev. Moon has brought back a notion to America which did dominate our religious theology and our culture for some time. However, that original American optimism (to build the Kingdom of God in communities on the Atlantic seaboard) now seems lost beyond recall.

When we come to the question of the Advent of the Messiah and the Mission of Jesus, there are many questions about Divine Principle doctrine. But the central issue, where God is concerned, is whom God chooses as his instruments. We are told that our mission is to find the central figure of the new history in order to unite with him. However, God did not foreknow Jesus' death, only its possibility. Both he and Jesus had to adjust their program and settle for the lesser good of spiritual salvation, due to the unfaithfulness of the people in Jesus' time. The question is whether the new central figure can turn human failure around. However, perhaps we can best see the issue of whom God chooses as instruments when *Divine Principle* states that Jesus came to sway the mighty, the leaders of his day, and not the outcasts he ended up with. "Actually, the disciples Jesus would have preferred were not people of this kind" (p. 160). The ignorant fishermen were such poor representatives, not such as to impress the powers that be. Jesus (and God) needed to win over the intellectual and political leaders of the day as followers in order to establish the full physical kingdom, marry and restore the family back to God's control.

In many ways, the issues concerning God come to a head at this point. Although churches have and often do adopt a triumphal and aristocratic mode, the gospel as traditionally preached stresses God's identification with the poor and the suffering and those not in the seats of power. It is not that the Unification Church neglects such; the Kingdom of Heaven is for all. But they see God's chance for success as necessitating a move through the power circles of the day. The lords of the earth, the scientists, the intellectual leaders and the respectable people, must join the movement of Principle if the Kingdom is to come on earth. This is why the church is open to criticism for the money it spends on real estate, industries, and the conferences of "important people" it sponsors on a lavish budget. They do engage in what traditional Protestants call social work, but it is consistent with their doctrine that the uncompleted work of Jesus demands that friends be won at high places at all levels of society. The social, political and financial operations of the movement are in keeping with the Principle, once the mode of God's operations is understood.

The issue, of course, is whether God is like this and whether the coming of his Kingdom depends on this kind of goodwill mission into the upper reaches of industry, culture, and political affairs. When the invited visitor arrived at Moon's Washington Monument rally held in September of 1976, in addition to receiving his fried chicken he witnessed several hours of entertainment, mostly by church member groups, capped by the world's largest fireworks display. In the middle of this, Rev. Moon appeared to speak for a time in Korean about God's plan for America, but the audience (except for church members) was bewildered. Considered in the light of the Principle, it all makes sense, and again it highlights the question of God's nature. Culture is being given back to God's purpose, and people should be swayed to join the rising tide. Members do not see themselves as a struggling band of outcasts but as the forefront of culture. True, the Principle predicts persecution and difficult times, but the goal is to infiltrate culture and society at all levels, after overcoming opposition, to succeed and win it back to God. Religion, then, seems less a matter of worship and more a matter of carrying the message to important people to gain their support.

Jesus had to settle for non-leaders on the social level, when he should have gone to Rome and won over the Roman Empire. But the question still remains: Does God work through, and require the cooperation of, the powerful in society? Is God's power so restricted that he must maneuver for support? Or, can he take the lowly, the despised, the unexpected and use weak reeds to accomplish his plan because his power is sufficient unto itself? The God of Principle is thoroughly modern in accepting contingencies and genuine human freedom. He is traditional in holding absolute sway over creation. But again, as with other modern theologies, God is limited in what he can accomplish alone. His own power is bound to the processes of nature. *Divine Principle* has its interpretation of what these historical processes are, but it no less restricts God to these avenues than do other natural theologies and theories of historical evolution or progress. As *Divine Principle* continues, the major part of its bulk is devoted to intricate historical analyses and outlines of dates and sequences. Obviously, they feel God is to be found at work here.

VII.

When we come to the doctrine of "indemnity" as outlined in *Divine Principle* we reach another crucial point in our understanding of the God of Principle. The physical resurrection of Jesus is rejected as unacceptable to the modern mind (p. 165). The goal is the restoration of all humanity, so that the resurrection of one human body is unimportant. How does God accomplish this general restoration? Again, he is bound by Principle which requires that indemnity be paid for man's debt of sin (p. 186). Jesus has not "paid it all," as the hymn declares. Man must set up a corresponding condition of indemnity, although he may win the cooperation of the spirit world. The progression will go from the family level, to the national, and then to the worldwide level, but indemnity must be paid at each stage of advance. The question is whether God is a careful and unforgetting banker who counts the debt and checks the payments received. Or, in traditional terms, is he instead a God of grace who can forgive without demanding payment? If not, it is a fearful burden Moonists carry on their shoulders.

Again, in the section on Predestination we get a glimpse into the God of Principle. Evil is entirely due to man's failure to fulfill his portion of responsibility. God wills to accomplish his purpose in creation, but this can be fulfilled "only by man's accomplishment of his portion of responsibility" (p. 192), although this does include the work of the central figure in charge of the mission too. Thus, God is man-dependent, and, should man fail again as he has in the past, God's purpose fails. The crux of the matter is that Unificationists think the revelation of the Principle, plus something propitious in the culmination of events in the Last Days, make the success of the project likely today which has not been the case before. Some of God's previous failures were due to man's ignorance of God's principle, which has now been corrected. But still we have to ask: What if man fails again; will God fail? And, are the events of this day in fact so changed? Principle is clear in stating that the odds of success are indeed better today. Furthermore, should we fail again, can God overlook indemnity and failure and save us in spite of ourselves, or is his power really totally bound to Principle?

God's intention is absolute, but the accomplishment of his will is relative, we are told (p. 198). And it is here that the famous formula appears: God's ninety-five percent responsibility combined with man's five percent responsibility. The issue is not to debate the mathematics of these figures but to ask whether, if God's intention is absolute, must he not retain the power to accomplish his purpose even if the relative or contingent factors combine to force a loss again? One need not deny contingency in human affairs in order to assert God's power, as some have thought they must. The point is whether God retains any options if contingent events prove destructive in their outcome. God evidently has "omniscience" to the extent of being able to pick the central figure in the providence of restoration but not in the usual sense of foreknowing all events. The issue is mirrored in the question of Christology too. Jesus "can by no means be God himself" (p. 211), but the question is not so much the metaphysical one of Jesus' nature, or even God's complete foreknowledge, but whether Jesus retains God's full power to triumph over the tragedies which the contingencies of human existence lead to. Jesus does not need to be God, but he does need God's power.

Again, the *Divine Principle* doctrine of True Mother (and True Father) leads us to an insight into God's nature. The Holy Spirit is a female spirit (p. 215) and must come as the second Eve. Thus, to complete the duality in God, and to establish the four position foundation, "there must be a True Mother, along with the True Father, in order to give rebirth to the fallen children as children of goodness" (*Ibid.*). Whatever Rev. Moon's relation to the Principle, or whatever the office of the Lord of the Second Advent may be, it is clear that members regard him as the central figure of providence in the present age, and that he and Mrs. Moon are seen as True Father and True Mother in the process of restoration. Since this is the new truth revealed in the Principle, it is easy to see why Jesus should have married and established a family, and why restoration even now must follow this process. It traces back to the duality of male and female to God, and thus it is in all things and must be expressed in creation and be part of any true revelation of God. The New Testament does not speak in these terms, but, knowing God's plan as we do now in its entirety, we see that Jesus did not live long enough to reveal this part of the Principle. Thus, it is missing in the New Testament accounts.

When we are told that "man must set up certain necessary

conditions in order to restore himself" (p. 224), we realize that God reveals this principle (only fully in the Last Days) but man must accomplish it. God works on a partnership basis. In so doing he subjects himself to human failure, although *Divine Principle* is optimistic about the outcome this time around. The crucial factor is to know precisely God's heart, but this the Lord of the Second Advent reveals. Moonists are aware that human action in the past has failed. They document these repeated tragedies, or partial successes. But our ability to know God's heart now is what they count on to reverse this history of human failure. They believe the way has been opened to success, and now we must decide whether this seems to be so and whether we see God acting in terms of Principle. The foundation must be set up to receive the messiah if the mission is not to fail again. This, they say, cannot be accomplished by God's power alone, but is to be fulfilled "by man's joint action with God" (p. 283).

VIII.

When *Divine Principle* tells us that "God cannot grant man grace unconditionally" (p. 341), we know that God's power is bound by the procedures of the Principle. *Divine Principle* goes on to explain that this is because God does not want Satan to accuse him of unfairness. But surely this evidences a restricted God. (Why should God care what Satan says?) John the Baptist looms as the figure in the failure of Jesus to restore the full Kingdom, which again indicates how dependent God is on certain human actions. The course is set, and even God cannot alter it. It is a scenario given by God but acted out by men. "The Lord of the Second Advent must restore through indemnity the providential course of restoration left unachieved at the time of the first coming" (p. 364). God evidently has no other choice. "God's form is also mathematical" (p. 381), so that numerology looms large in interpreting and plotting God's actions. He is addicted to significant numbers and evidently bound in his actions by them. He likes 4, 21, 40 and 12. We can calculate his actions in such figures and their combinations.

God is a politician too, as well he must be, and he identifies with democracy (p. 442). After the monarchical image of God that domi-nated divine imagery for centuries, it is refreshing to find a democratic model, but it is perhaps too literally tied to existing political systems and ideologies. Satan steers us to communism. But the Second Advent of the Messiah must make the present political system display its intended function centered on God's will (p. 471), which contrasts dramatically with Jesus' aloofness from the politics of his day. But this was his mission's failure, according to *Divine Principle*. Jesus never got as far as his political and social program.

The history of evil's sovereignty centering on Satan is said to end with the appearance of the Lord of the Second Advent (p. 476). However, it is hard to see how this can be asserted so confidently, since God cannot accomplish this change with certainty by himself. *Divine Principle* answers: God will let the prophets know the day and the hour of the coming of the Lord of the Second Advent (p. 497), but the question is, why? Why must God share this secret, and can he know it with assurance in advance, given the restrictions on his own power of actualization? Korea is said to be the Third Israel (p. 521).

Young Oon Kim asserts that the "universe reflects the personality of God" (p. 3).[3] The universe becomes God's body, and since God's nature involves polarity, the creation and nature exist in the same polarity. Of course, this is not an empirical matter since the Fall makes man unlike God in that respect. This means you cannot see God by looking at man and nature directly but only in the "original mind" hidden within. Still, basic polarity is a primary feature of God, Kim says, and our problem is to evaluate this as a basic structure for understanding God. The inner invisible nature versus the outer form is a metaphysical structure which characterizes both God and his crea-tion. Subject, as the initiating force, and object, as the responding power, is another bi-polar mode for understanding God. The "four position foundation" is not so much a structure characteristic of nature as a form which prescribes relationships. "Give and take" also governs relationships. "The universal source energy emanating from God operates to stimulate and produce a give and take action between subject and object" (p. 11).

What shall we say about this metaphysical scheme for understanding God and his creation? Its value will eventually be determined by its use or disuse, but it is a "modern metaphysics," although derived from ancient sources. It has some counterparts in other suggestions about God, particularly either Process Theology or those based on an evolutionary scheme. It is, then, a viable framework for interpreting God, although, as I have argued, the metaphysics is not so important as the way in which God's actions are described according to Principle. However on one important score, that is, the protection of freedom and contingency in both God and man, Unification theory does better than most classical metaphysical schemes in Western theology, many of which start with a preference for necessity and completion, for example, Aristotle and Aquinas. When theologies derived from these principles want to interpret "freedom," they either have difficulty, because that notion runs counter to their metaphysical base, or they offer freedom in only a limited sense. The Principle makes freedom and contingency both basic and natural, which has advantages in the modern world.

Since God as the ultimate subject "requires an object for the give and take of his love" (p. 18), God cannot experience joy without the creation of nature and man within it. Some classical theologies asserted God to be dependent on nothing else, the sole absolute existent. Casting God with human qualities, particularly emotion, *Divine Principle* makes the creation of our natural order a necessity for God. However, Christian theologies have always come close to the assertion of the necessity of creation, so a metaphysical scheme which links God's own experience of completion with creation and its perfection can fit a Christian scheme. In many ways it is easier than theologies which work laboriously to prevent saying God required nature as an object of his love. It is, in fact, easy for *Divine Principle* to assert love in God as an emotion, as well as suffering. How to do this is a problem which has plagued Christian theologies for centuries, since they wished to assert God's love for man and his willingness to suffer in Jesus, but at the same time tried to protect his independence. However, like other contemporary theologies, Principle compromises

God's power in order to assert these features, so much so that he becomes dependent on the outcome of history.

Man and God become partners in moral and intellectual development (p.24). Man is challenged to become a co-creator. This enhances the significance of man, but it also compromises the control of God, as I have argued. Classical theologies tried to prevent this, even at the expense of adopting metaphysical notions which worked against such Christian principles as love and freedom. Heaven must begin on earth, we are told for example (p. 30). But this ties God to the outcome of the historical process. "The center of Unification theology is to alleviate God's sorrow and to fill his heart with happiness" (p. 35). That is an exhilarating and exciting task for men, but what if they fail? What if the formula of the Principle does not work? What can God do to avoid catastrophic loss? One who is optimistic about the outcome of culture need not worry about this, but what is the evidence that the human drama will in fact turn out to be comedy rather than tragedy on its own power? The Unification view of God offers options for man's freedom and an openness of history to contingency which other theologies have had difficulty affirming. But what about God's power in the face of human failure?

This question concerning God's power is illustrated again in *Divine Principle*'s account of the Fall and the centrality it is given. Of course, there is the question of whether the Fall should be so central in Christian theology and also whether Genesis should be given such a literal interpretation. But Kim is quite clear in wanting to keep God free of responsibility for the Fall. "God is in no sense a responsible participant" (p. 62). However, what God does not share in he may not have control over. That is, if in the beginning he could not recognize evil as part of his plan of creation, as Kim asserts, God was rather limited and blind not to be aware of what would become so central to the human drama and occupy his own energy for centuries. Man is left "to discern evil and abolish it by the exercise of his own free will" (p. 63). True, we had not been given the formula of the Principle until recently, and we ought to give its program time to prove itself. But a God innocent of evil also becomes dependent on man for its cure, and surely the human record to date does not hold out much optimism, given the demise of our confidence in evolution, progress, and trust in modern science. Divine Principle banks a lot on a dramatic reversal taking place in the present age. If it does not come about, what can the God of Principle do?

Just as Moonists believe that "a forthright and unqualified endorsement of Jesus by the Baptist would have turned the tide in Jesus' favor" (p. 98), so they still think a turn in political events is crucial in God's ability to establish his Kingdom today. Some in Jesus' time clearly expected him to make political moves to restore Israel's independence, and they were furious and dismayed when events did not move that way. Divine Principle retains this hope but moves its fulfillment up to the present day. What can God do if he is frustrated again? According to the Principle nothing except "try, try again"? "Without support, Jesus could not hope to lay a foundation for a godly Kingdom" (p. 103), that is quite right. But if Jesus failed to do this, as Moonists and other Christians agree, what can God do? The traditional version has God's power step in at the resurrection event, but Unificationists turn Jesus' resurrection into an account of the plan for historical restoration. At this point they are quite similar to Process Theology. But is God limited to these options, and is he always forced to follow men?

"God works in History," Kim says (p. 223), and when you read the account of God's operations in Divine Principle you find a God very much a stickler for detail, jealous and demanding, but little forgiving. His suffering and his love are clearly evident, but he is little able to do much about this except to keep working intricate schemes hoping to swing men to his side. "By the crucifixion of the Messiah of Israel," Kim tells us, "God's will was effectively thwarted" (Ibid.). Christianity has traditionally said that God did not accept Jesus' defeat and offered the resurrection as our hope. Unification theology does not accept this, and that does make it easier to account for why so little is changed in the world since Jesus' time. Some Christian traditions act too much as if the world were already changed as a result of Jesus' resurrection, when clearly little in the human condition has altered since the Jerusalem trial. On the other hand, if God was thwarted then and could or would do nothing about it (Moon and the Christian tradition agree that Jesus was his highest hope), what leads us to think that the future will be any more favorable to God's hope? Here we face the Principle. Is it so powerful that its formula can bring in the full Kingdom on earth and prevent God's failure this time?

Is "the inexorable march to goodness" (p. 253) as relentless as *Divine Principle* suggests? Here we face *Divine Principle*'s romantic and evolutionary-progress optimism. "According to the *Divine Principle*, in our own time we are witnessing a dramatic reversal of the direction of human events" (p. 256). That is fine, if true, but what can the God of Principle do if such optimism is not borne out? Are a new heaven and a new earth appearing? Most voices now speak of the spoiling of the earth and its devastation in the present age. Is love today increasing so that we now have the ability to "love as God loves"? (p. 258) The contemporary world talks more of holocausts. At this time in history, will "the spiritual and physical become one" (p. 261)? Will goodness steadily rise and evil decline? The Jews of Jesus' time expected this too, but it didn't happen. Is our time so different that we can succeed where others failed?—that is the question. Through a man and a truth, is world harmony "within our grasp" (p. 288)? That is fantastic if true. But does the God of Principle have a contingency plan if tragedy strikes human optimism again?

IX.

What, then, should our "critical appraisal" of the God of Principle be? (1) In explaining what he/she is like, I have asked the important questions in that context at each step. (2) In outlining how the God of Principle acts, I have also raised the issue of the limitation which Principle places on his action. (3) If I am right, it is not so much a question of a metaphysical appraisal of the technical concepts Moonists use to describe God's nature (e.g., polarities) as one of assessing the picture given of how such a God acts religiously. (4) Like all theologies, Unification thought should in the end be tested by the vigor of the religious life it creates and sustains. My assumption is that there is no one single "true" theology but a variety of ways to describe God, some more effective in certain situations than others. Moonists have stressed the peculiar crisis, the turning point of the present day. Many of the excesses the movement engages in, which have brought down a hail of criticism, stem from their sense of urgency that the time for men and women to move is now. Couple this with the conviction that man's role is crucial for either bringing in God's Kingdom or delaying it, and you have the makings of a crusade.

However, more important than an appraisal of either the original doctrine, or their present campaign to bring the Kingdom of God on earth, is the question of what the movement will do and how the doctrine may be revised if the projected time table does not hold or men fail the central figure again. This is a religious movement and a theology in its formation stage, to borrow a phrase from *Divine Principle.* Thus, its critical appraisal eventually depends more on how it is developed in the future than on assessing its past record or even its present (controversial) performance. Christianity was not built in a day. Of course, the movement could fade away, but that remains to be seen. I have argued:4 (1) that the movement is here to stay, although perhaps in lesser numbers than Moon hopes; and (2) that it is presently passing through its "crucifixion stage." Their crucial test will be, as for the early Christians, how the members respond to disappointed hopes, if they remain loyal and do not desert.

However, since our concern is the God of Principle, our question becomes: What will, or can, the God of Principle do if the present time table does not hold? Of course, since Moonists believe in a necessary growth stage, in human freedom, in contingency in human events, and the necessity for human cooperation according to a strict plan for restoration to succeed—failure or postponement is no surprise to them or to the God of Principle. He and they have borne disappointment, suffering and delay before. Thus, although they have a program, its frustration is not as difficult a matter for those who understand Principle as it would be for a Calvinist deterministic God. Furthermore, Rev. Moon has indicated that he may revise the present version of the *Divine Principle.* Neither he nor his followers consider it an infallible book, just as they do not accept every page of our present Bible literally. The question is whether the core of Principle can remain and the calendar built around it still be altered or changed. This is a process many religions, particularly millennial groups, have gone through in the history of both Judaic and Christian messianic expectations.

But will the God of Principle change any in the process? The terms in which he is described are not sacrosanct. If he did not close revelation with the fixing of the canon of the New Testament, he could speak again to Rev. Moon or to others. God's response to the lack of fulfillment of the *Divine Principle* program is almost more crucial than that of Rev. Moon or his followers. Yet God never speaks directly but only through human instruments, so the form in which we receive his word is fragile and our hearing is never perfect. "We have our treasures in earthen vessels." Religions which immunize themselves against change often crush themselves on their own inflexibility. Like Christianity, Unification thought incorporates many of the culturally popular notions of its time of origin. This does not prove it wrong but only that, like everything born in enthusiasm and pentecostal fervor, it needs refining. Some theologians refine away the core of their belief, using yet another more current set of cultural assumptions to replace the ones from an earlier time that they do not like. The question is whether the God of Principle can survive the refining fire which the-God-beyond-the-Principle seems to send to test every new incarnation.

However, as human beings, we come to know God by perceiving how he works. Where the vision of *Divine Principle* is concerned, the major issue is whether God works more through the major, the important, and the powerful figures in an era; or does he find the lowly, the humble, and the social outcast his preferable vessel? Christianity has in its theology traditionally stressed the latter, although like any institutional religion, in its practice it often cultivates the rich and the powerful. The Principle corrects the picture that the New Testament gives of the band of lowly fishermen made powerful by God's action. They say that the stress on the poor and the meek is simply the early church's apology for its failure to become successful and powerful, move on to challenge Rome and usher in God's Kingdom. The issue, however, is not to debate the question of New Testament interpretation or Divine Principle's special hermeneutic, but to ask ourselves how and where we find God active. This is the question Divine Principle raises for us.

Considering what we know about human nature, the powerful and successful seldom make good spiritual instruments, because they are too "full of themselves." Each has an agenda of his own, or he would not have climbed as far as he has. Those outside the power structure, those who lack temporal authority, are open and receptive to be filled by power outside themselves. "The well have not need of a physician." The Spirit can enter and find a home. It more easily transforms life in one who is not bound up with his or her own importance. In looking at the God of Principle, and as we seek to locate where God may be present in our own time, we need to ask what kind of human instrument God is likely to choose. Of course, both Rev. Moon and Korea were humble in their origins and lacking in world power as they emerged on the scene. But the issue is whether God next needs the help of "world leaders" as those who have been chosen to usher in his Kingdom move out from their early obscurity.

How could it have occurred to anyone that the way to usher in God's Kingdom on earth is to enlist the world's temporal authorities in the cause? At this point we come up against the element of shamanism in Unification thought. As I went to Korea to investigate the origins of the movement, the church's opponents repeatedly told me that Divine Principle was simply "Korean shamanism dressed up." I puzzled about this, particularly as I came to see Moon's Presbyterian missionary background and Divine Principle's close affinity with, and dependence on, Christian doctrine. But Moonists believe in an active spirit world. Rev. Moon has traveled there to meet the sages of the past and to do battle with the forces of Satan. He even talks of using the power of the spirit world in order to guide his church after his physical death. The battles in that world are decisive for the turn of events on this earth—that is the shamanistic element in Divine Principle.

Thus, Unification Family members count on spirit men to assist them in their labors on earth. This gives them confidence that they can win over to their cause otherwise self-preoccupied temporal power figures. Spirit men and women will come down to sway those decisive to victory, they are sure.

But if this shamanistic view of the power of the spirit world over our affairs is incorrect, and if God does not operate that way, the Principle is seriously in question. If God stands alone in his relation to affairs on this earth and seldom intercedes in human life, and if the spirit world is separated off from our own affairs more decisively than *Divine Principle* assumes, what then? God may still be present to us in the Holy Spirit, but Caesar's affairs would be his own and very little subject to spiritual influence. God would not correct the world and usher in his Kingdom by coercing powerful figures in the world of intellect, politics, and finance. He would work through the lowly and the meek, and by his own spiritual presence to those who seek him. That is, he works indirectly and in silence, until the day the trumpet is blown, and he breaks the power of the present temporal order by the direct release of his own power held in suspension for that decisive moment.

FOOTNOTES

[1]*Divine Principle* (Washington: Holy Spirit Association for the Unification of World Christianity, 1973).

[2]Young Oon Kim, *Unification Theology and Christian Thought* (New York: Golden Gate, 1975); see also Sang Hun Lee, "The Unification View of God," in Sebastian A. Matczak, ed., *God in Contemporary Thought* (New York: Learned, 1977), pp. 727-49.

[3]Kim.

[4]Frederick Sontag, *Sun Myung Moon and the Unification Church* (Nashville: Abingdon, 1977).

The Fall of Man
in *Divine Principle*

Francis Clark

On reading Divine Principle for the first time, I was especially struck by its coherence of structure and thought. To assess each of the individual chapters and sections aright it is necessary to see the work as a whole, and to realize how the individual parts fit into a master plan and how they mutually complement and clarify one another. Thus the meaning and force of the chapter on the Fall of Man is not fully apprehended until one has seen the application of the ideas here put forward in the later sections of the book. Moreover even the specific teaching on the Fall of Man is not restricted to the chapter on which I have been asked to comment. In several places in later chapters we return to the teaching on the Fall, and these later references bring new insight, and even at times a new choice of wording which throws light on what is said in our chapter.

It is right that I should "declare an interest" at the start, and indicate my own standpoint. I was for several years a Professor of Dogmatic Theology at the Pontifical Gregorian University, Rome. However, I hope my comments and my outlook will not be considered as too narrowly those of a Roman Catholic theologian and historian of Christian thought. My present responsibilities, and my own heart-felt interest, are concerned with the religious brotherhood of mankind in the widest sense. I learn much from the faith and worship of others, and I find I am enriched when I reverence the reverence of those who do not share my own belief.

For the sake of easy reference, and clarity in our discussion, I will group my comments under the headings of the Sections given in Chapter 2 of Part I of *Divine Principle*. I offer these reflections, for the most part, as questions. If I have not properly understood the original meaning of the text, perhaps it will be a useful occasion for others to point out what I have failed to apprehend.

Section I

It is indeed with a striking claim that this Section opens: "Until the present era, not a single man has known the root of sin". The same claim is repeated, in equivalent terms, later in the book. It will be a useful question to ask at the end of the discussion, how this claim is justified, and in what essential respects the answer given in *Divine Principle* is unique, in comparison with other answers given throughout history.

Does *Divine Principle* establish that man *is* fallen, or does it take this for granted? In the chapter on the Fall of Man, it seems to be taken for granted; nevertheless if we turn back to the General Introduction, we find the basic premise of the fallenness of man stated and justified there. In those opening pages of the book there is already sketched out a theology of "original righteousness", or, as it is there termed, "the original mind of man" as intended in the divine creative plan. The fact of the Fall is taken as certain. Texts from *Romans* witness to the universal experience of the "great contradiction in man"—namely, that, "within the same individual, the power of the original mind, which desires goodness, is at violent war against the power of the wicked mind, which desires evil" (DP, p.2).

In asserting this universal experience and conviction of the fallenness and evil inclinations of mankind, *Divine Principle* is at one with a fundamental teaching in mainstream Christianity from New Testament times, through the Augustinian tradition, through the witness of the Reformation, and still present both in Catholic and Protestant theology to this day. This teaching is also a constant in Eastern Orthodox Christianity, though there it is less prominent. If we ask whether this traditional Christian doctrine implies that the fallenness of mankind is so obvious from universal experience that it is naturally knowable, and known, even independently of the Christian scriptural revelation, we do not find unanimity among the theologians. Those in the Augustinian tradition would answer affirmatively. Fallen man inevitably experiences and knows his predicament, even if he cannot know without revelation and grace the divine answer to it. On the other hand, an influential trend in Mediæval and later Catholic theology, represented by the Franciscan, Scotist, Nominalist, Jesuit and other Molinist schools, would not necessarily answer in the affirmative. (For very different reasons, Karl Barth also denies that the reality of original sin can be comprehended independently of scriptural revelation.) As we shall see, these schools differed from the thorough-going Augustinian theology in their understanding both of the nature of original righteousness and of the effects of the Fall. Since they did not agree that human nature was radically vitiated by the Fall, they did not assert that the fact of fallenness could be certainly and universally deduced by all men from their experience of inescapable moral decadence.

Since we are discussing *Divine Principle* in comparison not only with mainstream traditional theology but also in comparison with other influential theological positions both in antiquity and in modern times, it is also relevant to point out that since the days of Schleiermacher there has been a significant rejection within the world of Protestant theology of the dogma of both the Fall and fallenness of man. Liberal Protestantism turned away from what it saw as the pessimistic Augustinian heritage, and asserted an evolutionary optimism. There was no state of original righteousness from which man had fallen; human waywardness and the moral struggle were to be attributed to the imperfections and obstacles inseparable from the upward march of evolutionary progress.

It is true that the sombre experience of two World Wars in the twentieth century brought a sharp check to this evolutionary optimism of Liberal Protestantism, and a return to a theology of crisis based on the Pauline and Augustinian insights. Yet we should recognize that in the wide field of modern theological thought the evolutionary perspective is once again a significant influence. Not only is it widespread in post-Barthian Protestantism, but it also has an important impact in Catholic theology, especially through the spread of the ideas of Teilhard de Chardin. Now *Divine Principle* claims to promote and provide a synthesis between faith and science; yet the ruling orthodoxy in science holds tenets about evolution which would seem to be difficult to reconcile with the premises of *Divine Principle* about the earliest condition of mankind and the Fall. I would like to hear this question further discussed. Later I shall refer again to the rival theories of monogenism and polygenism; whereas the latter is asserted by most biological scientists, *Divine Principle* seems to depend on acceptance of the former. Or is there some reconciliation of these two apparently conflicting viewpoints, which is not explicitly spelt out in *Divine Principle*?

Any theology of the Fall must presuppose a theology of creation and of original righteousness. This *Divine Principle* provides, in Chapter 1. We cannot discuss the teaching on the Fall without constantly referring back to the principles laid down in the previous chapter. I note here some points from that chapter which are very relevant to our present discussion. There is the affirmation on pp. 38-39: "Man was created to be the center of harmony of the whole macrocosm.... However, the universe lost this center when man fell; consequently, all of creation has been groaning in travail, waiting..." Although this conviction of the travail and disorientation of the whole material universe as a result of man's fall is not often asserted in modern Christian theology, it has considerable support from Patristic and later traditions.

Likewise the test to which the protoparents of the human race were put in their state of original righteousness, discussed in Section V of Chapter 1, is presented in a way which largely accords with much of Christian tradition. A notable exception is that in mainstream Christian tradition man was not cast for the role of ruler of the angels (cf. DP, p. 56 and p. 61).* The corollary, stated on p. 58, that "God does not dominate the world directly" is likewise untraditional from the

* There is, of course, I *Corinthians* VI.3.

standpoint of Christian theology. One may also remark in passing that the statement in the second paragraph on p. 56 seems akin to the view of the Semi-Pelagians about the *"initium fidei"* being man's contribution, and not the gift of God's grace. This is not to imply, of course, that *Divine Principle* must be bound by or interpreted in accordance with the categories of traditional Christian theology. I mention this and similar points of contrast because I take it that our purpose is to make a comparative appraisal of the text before us, and especially to note what is distinctive in it.

Turning now directly to the text of Section I of Chapter 2, I note with interest the exegesis of *Genesis* III which sees the two trees in the Garden of Eden as symbolizing respectively manhood and womanhood, the Tree of Life being associated with Adam and the Tree of Knowledge of Good and Evil being associated with Eve. Although, as I shall note later, there was a considerable body of opinion in ancient times which held that after the Fall women were given special occult knowledge by the demons, I do not find that this interesting symbolism of the two trees of Eden has any close parallel in the long history of scriptural exegesis.

The exposition of the significance of the serpent in the *Genesis* account, given on pp. 69-71, is wholly consonant with traditional interpretations. Note the rejection of dualism, in the insistence that the spiritual tempter described in the guise of a serpent is not "a being in existence before creation with a purpose contrary to that of God". If that were so, as in Manichæan and Gnostic dualism, and as in Zoroastrianism (according to a common interpretation) then, as *Divine Principle* puts it, "the struggle between good and evil in the world would be inevitable and eternal". As in all orthodox Christianity, *Divine Principle* sees Satan as a spiritual being "originally created for the purpose of goodness who later fell and was degraded". There is no deep root of pessimism in *Divine Principle*, as in those ancient world views which also stressed the pervasiveness of evil in the world. *Divine Principle* faces the problem of evil and gives it an arresting statement; but throughout there is a dominant stress on the goodness of crea-tion. Evil neither enters into the divine nature, nor is it an independent empire over against God, nor can it eventually thwart God's good purpose.

To assert the fallenness of mankind is not the same as to assert the actual event and circumstances of the Fall. Divine Principle proceeds to do the latter in considerable detail. To what extent are Unificationists constrained to accept this account as historical fact, and to what extent can they interpret it symbolically, so that they need not assert that any such events ever happened in time and on this earth? In asking this question, of course, one inevitably makes comparisons with similar preoccupations within modern Christian theology. Although the author of Divine Principle discards naively literal interpretations of some details of the Genesis narrative (e.g., that the fruit was literally a fruit, and that the transgression of Adam and Eve was literally through eating of that fruit), nevertheless he is very far from allegorizing away the whole drama of Eden. The persons in the drama are real individual persons, even though they have a cosmic significance. Although the actual nature of the events is outside our experience and is not readily imaginable as a pictorial scenario, there is no doubt from the text of the Divine Principle that the events actually happened, that they were physical happenings, and that they had dire physical consequences for the whole human race, and conditioned the whole of human history.

It is when we return to the remaining sub-sections in Section I, and the first two sub-sections of Section II (DP, pp. 71-80) that we find what is most distinctive in the teaching of Divine Principle about the Fall, and what is in most marked contrast with mainstream Christian theology. Yet strange as the account given here may seem to those who know only the mainstream Christian tradition, it is interesting to note that there are parallels to this teaching to be found in the history of Jewish and Christian speculation outside mainstream theology.

The interpretation of the Fall of the Angel, as being an act of fornication, has many echoes in ancient religious literature. Although Divine Principle refers only to Jude I.6-7, this text is by no means an explicit assertion that the rebel angels fell through lust. There are much more explicit and circumstantial statements in the Jewish apocryphal literature of the inter-testamental period. In this literature, and in a long posterity of writings dependent upon it, there is a special preoccupation with a "Fall of the angels", not based on *Genesis* III, but on *Genesis* VI.1-4: "And after that men began to be multiplied on the earth and daughters were born to them. The sons of God seeing the daughters of men, that they were fair, took to themselves wives of all which they chose.... Now giants were upon the earth in those days. For after the sons of God went in to the daughters of men, and they brought forth children, these are the mighty men of old...". In the apocryphal *Book of Enoch*, dating from about 170 B.C., there is an explicit explanation of the coming of evil into human experience, through interpreting *Genesis* VI.1-4 as relating a miscegenation between wayward angels and women. The "sons of God" were identified as the attendant angels called "watchers". When, bewitched by the beauty of women, they copulated with them, they thereby begot a new mixed lineage. Moreover the fallen angels, Azazel in particular, taught their human wives secrets of wickedness. Here sin is evil knowledge, not transmitted guilt. A similar interpretation of *Genesis* VI.1-4 is found in other apocrypha dating from between the second century B.C. and the first century A.D., including the *Testaments of the Twelve Patriarchs*, the *Book of Songs*, the *Book of Parables*, the *Book of Jubilees* (as interpolated) and the *Fourth Book of Ezra*. It was especially the *Book of Enoch* that had most effect on Christian thinkers in the first four centuries of the Christian era. It was widely supposed to be canonical, and for that reason many Fathers of the Church and ecclesiastical writers of repute repeated its fanciful embroidering of the events of *Genesis* VI.1-4. The interpretation of the text, which understood it to refer to a miscegenation between fallen angels and women, was given additional emphasis by a variant reading of the text of the Septuagint Greek translation of the Old Testament in verses 2 and 4 of that chapter. Instead of reading *"hoi huoi tou Theou"* this variant gave *"hoi angeloi tou Theou"*—that is, it was directly stated in this variant that it was "the angels of God" who went in to the daughters of men. This variant reading was for long the most widely accepted in the early Church. The Apologists of the second century found no difficulty in accepting the notion of carnal commerce between angelic spirits and women. For example St. Justin Martyr clearly knows the text of the *Book of Enoch* and the *Book of Jubilees*, and explains that the offspring of this unnatural union were the demons who tempt and prey upon men (*Apologia* II.5). The same tradition is continued by Athenagoras, Irenæus, and Clement of Alexandria, who held that although the angels partook of the spiritual world, they were capable of being attracted to a lower beauty. Likewise Tertullian calls these fallen angels *"desertores Dei, amatores feminarum"*, and uses this example to warn women against cosmetics and bewitching finery. Julius Africanus took the "daughters of men" to be the "daughters of the race of *Cain*". The Clementine apocrypha of the third century explained that after falling from their high estate into an illicit union with women the wicked spirits revealed to women evil arts such as idolatry, magic, astrology and other forms of human perversity. As in exegesis of the Eden story, so here there was a readiness to see women as especially connected with the origin of sin and evil. Lactantius explained that there were two kinds of demons; the first were spiritual creatures only, fallen from heaven; the others were the descendants of the perverse sexual union mentioned in *Genesis* VI. Although we already find a rejection of the *Book of Enoch* as non-canonical by Origen in the third century, we find a surprising survival of the ideas sprung from it right into the fourth and fifth centuries, even in the work of eminent Fathers such as St. Athanasius, St. Ambrose and St. Jerome. From the time of St. Augustine the philosophical refinement of the distinction between spirit and matter made it seem absurd to postulate a sexual union between angelic spirits and human beings. St. John Chrysostom denounced as a fable the story of the fornication of angels with the daughters of men, and from the fifth century onwards this tradition, sprung from the interpretation of *Genesis* VI.1-4 as interpreted in the Jewish apocrypha, disappeared from orthodox Christian exposition. It had also been present in Gnostic speculation, for example in Heracleon in the second century. It can still be traced, here and there, in obscurer writings of later centuries.

I have pointed out that the tradition I have just referred to, of a kind of fornication between fallen angels and the daughters of men, was not based on the temptation narrative in Eden of *Genesis* III, but on the subsequent text from *Genesis* VI. In this there is clearly a significant difference from the teaching of *Divine Principle*, which locates the original fornication of the Angel in Eden itself. Just as the Fall of the Angel is attributed to illicit intercourse between Satan and the first woman, so the Fall of the first man is also understood to have been a sexual sin. The explanation in *Divine Principle* is nuanced, and takes account of obvious objections which could be brought against this interpretation of *Genesis* III. Some of the indications which are given in *Divine Principle* to show that this sin of the protoparents of humanity was a sexual transgression were also used by writers in antiquity.

Strangely enough, there was much greater readiness in the early Church to admit illicit carnal union between angels and women in the post-Eden period than to explain the sin of Adam and Eve as an act of fornication. This idea was, it is true, sufficiently current to call forth protests and counter-proofs from the Fathers and Doctors of the Church. It seemed especially significant, as *Divine Principle* points out on p. 72, that after the Fall Adam and Eve became ashamed of their nakedness and covered their sexual parts. St. Augustine himself seems to find that this detail is somewhat surprising, since one would more naturally suppose that they would have covered their mouths, the organs through which they had sinned. Moreover, the maledictions delivered by God against the woman concerning the travails and sorrows of childbirth and maternity could be taken to indicate a link between her sin and her sexual function. (The serpent, too, had sexual connotations in the context of Canaanite fertility cults of which the Yahwist author would have been aware.) However, the Fathers, including both the Alexandrians and the Antiochenes, as well as the Fathers of the West led by St. Augustine, insisted that the Fall of our first parents was a sin of disobedience, and not of sexual disorder. The prohibition of God concerning the Tree of the Knowledge of Good and Evil, the Fathers pointed out, indicated a prohibited *knowledge*, and clearly laid down a divine precept which was a test of obedience and humility. The inspired author of *Genesis* had exalted marriage in his account of creation and of the divine ordinance; would he go on to represent the union of spouses as a sin? (*Divine Principle*, of course, has an answer to this objection. It was not married union as such that was prohibited, but its consummation at the wrong time, in the period of growth before it could come to proper fruition.) The punishment of the woman does not prove that the sin was sexual, any more than the divine malediction of the man or of the serpent relates to the nature of their guilt. The ordinary interpretation of the "fig leaf" sequel of the transgression of Adam and Eve was that concupiscence arose as a *consequence* of the preceding original sin which caused the Fall. St. Gregory of Nyssa even supposes that biological sex, and its use, arose only as a result of the Fall. The original God-like men, in their ideal state, would have multiplied in a fashion unknown to us, without the use of sex (De Hominis Opificio, 17). In later mainstream Christianity it was taken as established beyond dispute that the first sin of Adam and Eve was one of disobedience, a sin of the spirit, a rebellion of the human will against the divine will. To interpret it, as Divine Principle does, as "an improper act of love" between the intended spouses is not indeed unheard of in the long history of Christian thought, but it sharply contrasts with the accepted Christian theology of the past 1500 years. At the time of the Reformation, indeed, the notion reappeared, especially among sects of the Radical Reformation, and can still be traced in modern times.

In the sub-section entitled "The Act of Adultery between the Angel and Man", and in the further explanation given on the two following pages (DP, pp. 74-75), there is much to discuss, and I should like to know whether I have understood the teaching aright. Evidently there is a difficulty in admitting that there could be "an adulterous relationship between the angel and man". This primordial act, the evil union between Satan and Eve, is given great importance in Divine Principle, and one wants to be sure that one has understood both what is meant by the act and its consequences. Evidently it is not merely an improper union of will, through ill-regulated desire or consent; it is more than that, since the act is a physical or ontological union, and it has physical or ontological consequences of great importance. Phrases which need clear explanation here are, for example: "We have come to understand that the root of sin is not that the first human ancestors ate a fruit, but that they had an illicit blood relationship with an angel symbolized by a serpent"; "From this act, all men came to be born of Satanic lineage, apart from God's"; "What were the circumstances surrounding the affair which made man the descendant of the fallen angel, Satan?" These questions are to be further elucidated in the light of what we read in the following Sections.

Section II

The doctrine of the angels contained in sub-section 1 accords largely with traditional Christian belief. One may except the affirmation that the angels were created to assist God in the creation of the universe (although this doctrine does not lack some support from ancient and mediæval writers): likewise the affirmation that "man was supposed to dominate the angels, too".

In sub-section 2 we return to the problem of the illicit sexual relationship between Satan and Eve. Although we are told that this was "the spiritual fall" whereas the illicit relationship between Eve and Adam was "the physical fall", it is clear that according to the teaching of *Divine Principle* the first fall was not merely in the moral or intentional order. Feelings, sensations and contact can be predicated even of spiritual beings: "Therefore, sexual union between a human being and an angel is actually possible". On page 79 we read that "Eve received certain elements from Lucifer when she joined into one body with him through love". These elements are given as the sense of fear, leading to guilty conscience, and a kind of higher wisdom giving her insight into creative purpose. As I have observed above, there is an ancient, and quite long-continued tradition within the Christian Church, which saw no impossibility in an illicit carnal union between angels and women, leading even to the procreation of demonic offspring which partook of the nature of both parents. (I may also recall that even when such a notion was rejected as impossible in the official theology of the Church, the idea of actual sexual intercourse between a devil and a woman long continued in mediæval and later folklore—for example, in the popular dread of the Plantagenets as the "Devil's Brood". The mediæval doctors did not dispute that the devil in bodily guise could so invade the body of a woman, nor that she could be a willing accomplice in the unnatural union; but they denied that it could be true generation, since a spirit could not procreate from a human being.)

The description given in *Divine Principle* of the Spiritual Fall of Lucifer, in his illicit union with Eve, is free from the grossness of some ancient and mediæval speculations. The motivation which led Lucifer to tempt Eve to submit to him is of great interest. The explanation of this motivation has a resemblance to traditional Christian teaching that it was because of envy of man, newly created and highly endowed and loved by God, that the devil brought about man's Fall. In support of this view there was the text in the *Book of Wisdom* (accepted as canonical in the Catholic Church): "For God created man incorruptible, and to the image of his own likeness he gave him. But, by the envy of the devil, death came into the world" (II.23-24). One should note, however, that in traditional theology the devil had already fallen before he tempted Eve and Adam; whereas in *Divine Principle* the devil's fall was in the act of making the woman fall. The devil's sin was traditionally explained as basically a sin of pride, which led him to refuse to acknowledge the nobility of human nature, in which he was shown that God himself would become incarnate in Jesus Christ. This explanation, I should add, was never an official dogma of the Church, but a theological opinion widely held.

What is significantly different in the teaching of *Divine Principle* is that Lucifer saw in his seduction of Eve his opportunity and hope to use this contact with human nature so that he might obtain the mediatorship between God and the whole universe, in addition to the mediatorship he already possessed as the supreme archangel in the angelic world.

The motivation which led Eve to draw Adam into a premature and illicit sexual relationship is also described in a passage of great psychological interest. The consequences of the two-fold adultery are further explained later. The whole of this part of *Divine Principle* is very carefully constructed and closely argued; to understand the significance of the two-fold Fall in its cosmic context and consequences one has to return to the deep metaphysical foundations laid in Chapter 1, "Principle of Creation".

Section III

I find this short Section of particular importance, since it points to a basic premise which underlies the whole approach to reality put forward in *Divine Principle*. It is the assertion that the power of love is stronger than all, even stronger than the power of the Principle. There is a fundamental strength and soundness in a world-outlook which declares the primacy of love. Fate, necessity, eternal law—affirmation of these ultimates can undergird sombre, pessimistic and world-denying philosophies and theologies. But the affirmation of ultimate love is the avowal that life-bringing goodness is at the heart of all reality and act. *Bonum est diffusivum sui.* One is reminded of the mediæval controversies about the primacy of divine Will or Intellect. One is reminded, at a deeper level, of St. Paul's "the greatest of these is love", and of St. John's "God is love".

Section IV

The consequences of the Fall of man are here worked out with clarity and logical coherence. Understanding of these consequences is necessary for an understanding of the Restoration which is to be explained later in the book.

In sub-section 1 emphasis is laid on how "the world came under Satanic sovereignty". There is, indeed, scriptural warrant for this conviction, and it has played a large part in Christian thinking through the ages. It is strongly reasserted throughout *Divine Principle*, and it seems to be a powerful psychological element in the spiritual attitude of those who accept *Divine Principle* as their guide. There is no need to point out how alien this viewpoint must seem to the majority of their contemporaries, not only those who accept materialistic and secular assumptions, but also a large proportion of believing Christians in the modern age. They see it as a psychological and religious aberration of past ages to be obsessively preoccupied with the action of demons in the world, and they pass unfavourable judgments on past ages, such as the later Middle Ages and the period of the Reformation, when Christians were intensely concerned with the devil and with manifestations of diabolic power. Many Christians today either deny the existence of evil spirits, or at least hold that they should have no place in the religious consciousness of believers. Is there a danger that Unificationists give too much attention to the demonic and Satanic, and that by asserting that in some way human beings are descendants of Satan they are obscuring their assertion of the goodness of being and of the power of love? I realize that an answer can be given from the pages of Divine Principle itself (e.g., in sub-section 3, pp. 85-87); but it is an answer which needs to be discussed.

I have some incidental questions about points raised on page 86. There we read, in the second paragraph, "that even the world of evil, when turned towards the purpose of goodness centered on Christ, will be restored to perfect goodness, thus realizing the Kingdom of God on earth". This belongs rather to later stages in our discussion, when we consider the teaching on the Restoration. But in passing I ask whether there is here a hint of the doctrine, put forward in antiquity by Origen and a few others, which held that even Satan and his fallen angels would eventually be saved in the final restoration of all things?

I find the last paragraph on page 86, continuing on to page 87, obscure. Is the English translation perhaps to blame?

Another point on which I should like clarification is the teaching about "the spirit men of evil men on earth" (p. 84). Sub-section 4, on "The Works of Good Spirits and Evil Spirits" is relevant here. Are "the evil spirit men" permanently such, or do men who are at other times collaborating with the work of good spirits become temporarily "evil spirit men" when they collaborate with the work of evil spirits? I may note in passing that sub-section 4 has a number of resemblances to a famous section of the Spiritual Exercises of St. Ignatius Loyola, entitled "On the Discernment of Spirits".

The definition of the four kinds of sins, given in sub-section 5 (pp. 88-89), may usefully be discussed. I note there is a distinction between "original sin", defined as "the sin derived from the spiritual and physical fall of the first human ancestors", and, on the other hand, "hereditary sin", which is defined as "the sin of the ancestors transmitted to the descendants through blood lineage". This distinction of two kinds of derived sin, one derived from the first parents of the human race, and the other presumably derived from less remote ancestors, seems unusual. It could be objected that the text from *Exodus* XX.5, cited in *Divine Principle* at this point, does not say that the sin of the parents will be *conveyed* through several generations, but that the iniquity of the fathers will be *visited* upon the children to the third and fourth generation of those who hate God. The third kind of sin distinguished in this sub-section, namely "collective sin" is one that is much discussed in modern theology. Many theologians equate a collective "sin of the world" with what older theology described as original sin.

In this connection, I may observe that the view, widely accepted in modern Christian theology, that the account in *Genesis* III is not a divine revelation that there was an initial Fall involving individual protoparents of the whole human race, but is a symbolic assertion of the universality of "collective sin", is not only in opposition to *Divine Principle* but also to the traditional teaching of the Christian Church and the universal belief of the faithful throughout the greater part of Christian history. It is also in opposition to the teaching still maintained by the ordinary *magisterium* of the Roman Catholic Church (as can be seen in the Encyclical *Humani Genesis* of Pope Pius XII and in a later pronouncement by Pope Paul VI), and to the biblical understanding of many other Christians, notably the Eastern Orthodox and many in the Protestant Churches. On this point we do not find *Divine Principle* ranged over against mainstream Christian theology, but rather in the same camp with traditional mainstream theology. Thus the same criticisms which are levelled against conservative Catholic and Evangelical theology, for being "fundamentalist" and "outmoded", will naturally be made by many modern theologians against the Unificationist interpretation of *Genesis* III and of the doctrine of original sin.

However, because the perspective of *Divine Principle*, like that of conservative Christian theology, is now dismissed as old-fashioned, that is no reason for denying it serious consideration. Fashions in theological thinking vary from age to age, and a *Zeitgeist* can change remarkably in a fairly short span of time. An example was the great swing of the pendulum when Liberal Protestantism waned in the first part of the twentieth century, and neo-orthodoxy became the most dynamic movement within Protestant theology. It would be rash to assume that the present near-abandonment of the doctrine of original sin will necessarily be permanent; in a future age it may be restored to centrality in Christian theology.

The last sub-section in Section IV is entitled "The Original Nature of the Fall". Some very controversial questions, which have exercised the minds of Christian theologians throughout the centuries, are relevant to a discussion of this brief sub-section, interpreted in the light of what has preceded it. What are "all the characteristics" which were transmitted from Lucifer to Eve, then from Eve to Adam, and so "gave rise to the fallen nature of man"? On page 79 the only two "elements" mentioned, as received by Eve from Lucifer in her illicit act of love with him, were the sense of fear and wisdom concerning her intended spouse. Nevertheless, it is clear from several references throughout *Divine Principle* that "the fallen nature of man" implies the influence of considerably more than these two "elements".

The "fallen nature of man", stemming from the inherited characteristics, is evidently something positive and intrinsic to man, containing active propensity to evil. There is wide scope for discussion of this point, to ask how the teaching of *Divine Principle* stands in relation to the historic controversies between theologians about the nature and constituents of transmitted original sin. While the teaching of *Divine Principle* is clearly more "optimistic" about the fallen nature of man than is the thorough-going Augustinian teaching of total corruption, it would also seem that it would not go so far as the opinion, predominant in Roman Catholic theology since the Middle Ages, according to which original sin is essentially a privation, the absence of something (namely, sanctifying grace) which ought to be there according to the original endowment by which God raised man's natural capacities to a supernatural destiny.

Again, *Divine Principle* does not enter into the question, so hotly debated in past centuries, about the manner of transmission of original sin. Clearly, it agrees with the traditional teaching, reaffirmed both by the Protestant Reformers and by the Council of Trent, that original sin was transmitted by the process of human generation, and not merely by moral influence or imitation. The opinion of St. Augustine, that it was the human procreative act precisely as affected by lust that was the causal instrument for the transmission of original sin is not here asserted in such terms. Is something similar implied in what we read on pages 75-76, about adultery as the root of sin, about the significance of circumcision, about the "evil blood" received because of universal adultery, and about the inevitability of this evil inclination in all humanity up to the time of the Lord of the Second Advent?

The notion of "concupiscence" has a wider significance in Christian theology than disordered sexual desire, and *Divine Principle* clearly does not restrict the evil inclination in man to sexual disorder. One may ask how Unificationist theology would stand in relation to the vexed historical controversies about the place of concupiscence in original sin: whether it is identical with transmitted original sin, as Luther held, or whether it is a partial ("material") element of it, as Aquinas held, or whether it is not a constituent element of it at all, but merely a penal consequence, as the Scotists, Nominalists and Molinists held?

Section V

The discussion here about human freedom in the various phases of man's existence also has analogies with parallel discussion in traditional theology about freedom in the supralapsarian, infralapsarian and eschatological phases. *Divine Principle* seems to be in accord with the stricter Augustinian tradition, and with Reformation theology, in asserting that "man lost his freedom because of the fall" (p.93). This absolute-sounding assertion is, however, mitigated by the statement that follows, to the effect that "man, though fallen, still has a remainder of his original nature which seeks freedom in God", and further, "that, as time goes by, man's zeal for the pursuit of freedom grows". It would be anachronistic to interpret these statements in terms of the classic debates about free will and divine determinism; but at least they offer some analogies with both Arminian and Roman Catholic teaching, even if they do not go so far as the Council of Trent, which anathematized any who asserted that "after the sin of Adam the free will of man was lost and extinguished" (Canon 5 *de iustificatione*).

A noteworthy feature of this Section of *Divine Principle*, not found in any of the traditional views mentioned above, is the teaching that the tendency and the yearning for "the freedom of the original mind" has been renewed and developed in the course of time. "In the providence of restoration" it seems that this hunger and zeal for freedom is pointing forwards to its fulfilment. The social revolutions of recent centuries are not said to be a legitimate part of this providential process, but at least they testify to the growing strength of man's yearning for his original freedom.

Section VI

The deep questions raised in this Section cannot be brushed aside as mere anthropomorphism, or as mere metaphysical subtleties. They involve the problem of evil itself, the radical search for a theodicy which perpetually presses on the religious conscience of mankind, and which all the world religions seek to answer in one way or another.

Why did God, although omniscient and omnipotent, "not intervene to prevent the act of the fall when He foresaw it"? *Divine Principle* says that this basic question "has been left unsolved throughout human history". One may understand this assertion to mean that none of the solutions proposed are considered satisfactory. In Christian theology many great minds have offered partial solutions, but there is a readiness to admit that the full resolution of this mysterious question lies beyond the adequate grasp of human reason.

Although modern theologians would refuse to discuss the question in the categories presented here, theologians of past centuries, especially the mediæval scholastics and the Calvinist thinkers of the sixteenth, seventeenth and eighteenth centuries, would have acknowledged that this way of presenting and discussing the question was meaningful and useful. The Scotist and Ockhamist theologians who distinguished *momenta rationis* in the divine will and providential decrees, were well aware that this kind of distinction referred to ontological priority, not to temporal sequence or multiplicity, which could have no place in the being of God. Nevertheless they, like Protestant theologians later who discussed the order of the divine decrees, found this form of theological speculation a necessary path to a deeper penetration of the divine mystery. The use of similar processes of reasoning in *Divine Principle* when discussing the counsel and volition of God can likewise be defended from the charge of anthropomorphism.

Of the three reasons given in this Section, the first, namely that God did not intervene to prevent the Fall in order not to circumvent the free responsibility he had delegated to man, can be found not only in the thinking of Pelagians but also in some Catholic thinkers of later centuries. The second reason would be countered by most Christian speculative theologians, on the grounds that God's permissive will does not implicate him either in causality of or in responsibility for the moral evil attending some physical act. Moral evil as such requires no positive cause, since it is a negation, a falling away from due goodness, a "surd", as Lonergan puts it.

As for the third reason in this Section, it depends on the metaphysical postulates about divine and created dominion which were set out in the previous chapter. Those who accept the postulates in question will find the present reasoning cogent; those who do not will likewise be unconvinced here.

Some Concluding Reflections on "The Fall of Man"

In its interpretation of Chapters II and III of *Genesis*, *Divine Principle* succeeds better than the usual Christian expositions, it seems to me, in giving coherence to the divine prohibition, given originally to Adam and Eve, not to eat of the Tree of the Knowledge of Good and Evil. The Yahwist author presents the act of eating from that tree as an act of *enlightenment*, and he indicates that man acquired a faculty of discernment by his act of disobedience. It would be a relevant difficulty to bring against the ordinary Christian exegesis to object that according to Christian doctrine the Fall did not bring enlightenment or enhanced discernment, but ignorance and moral obfuscation.

I have already noted the strong impression given by *Divine Principle* of a creed which is optimistic, positive and life-affirming. There are some significant phrases on page 86: "...the purpose of creation was to obtain joy, and joy can be obtained only when desire is fulfilled. If man had no desire or ambition, he could have no joy". This is in direct opposition to creeds which show man's ultimate goal as reached by the part of the extinction of desire. The perspectives of *Divine Principle* are very different from those of Stoicism, Quietism or Buddhism.

Nevertheless, *Divine Principle* is also in opposition to exaggerated evolutionary optimism, which would see the moral obliquity of man as no more than imperfection and defectibility inherent in the process of evolution from a state of primitive struggle towards higher consciousness. "Misuse of human liberty is one thing: it is involved in original sin. But the misuse revealed is one that brings with it a privation of godliness, which is not identical with defective creaturehood" (C.J. Peter).

When referring earlier to evolutionary theory, I said that I would return to the problem of monogenism. Like the traditional Christian theology of original sin, *Divine Principle* has to face the widespread assumption that belief in an individual pair of human protoparents, as the starting point of the "history of salvation", is incompatible with science. To put the objection in a nutshell: "The appearance of an individual mutant is not evolution; only populations evolve and survive, not individuals" (E. Bone, *Nouvelle Revue Théologique*, 1962). Some Christian theologians deny that this dictum of science can determine what happened at the dawn of human spiritual responsibility; since human evolution is unique, a special teleology can be assumed for it. Others accept the postulate of polygenism, and adopt a symbolic interpretation of *Genesis* which they see as compatible with it. According to Karl Rahner and others, such a reinterpretation is not excluded for

Roman Catholic theologians, even by the papal Encyclical, *Humani Generis*. How would Unificationists view a similar enterprise to reinterpret *Divine Principle* in a polygenistic perspective?

The great value of discussions such as the one on which we are at present engaged is, in my opinion, that they insistently redirect the attention of Christian thinkers to the revealed doctrine of original sin, which has during the past century become a largely neglected branch of theology, relegated to the limbo of unimportant or outmoded opinions. This doctrine of original sin runs counter to so much of what is taken for granted in modern thought, so that, to quote Karl Rahner, "It is understandable but not on that account excusable that the doctrine plays a very small part in the contemporary presentation of Christianity". It is now fifty-six years since N.P. Williams, in the first of his Bampton Lectures, described the contemporary theological situation in terms which are even more applicable to the situation today:

> "There was a time when the scheme of orthodox dogma appeared to all as an unshakeable adamantine framework, reposing upon the two pillars of the Fall and of Redemption. These two complementary conceptions—that of the great apostasy, which defaced the image of God in man, and that of the great restoration through the Incarnation and the Atonement, which renewed it—were universally taken for granted as the twin focal points which determined the ellipse of traditional theology.... It is not too much to say that, whilst for professed and genuine Christians the second great pillar of the faith, the doctrine of Redemption, remains unshaken, founded upon direct experience of the redeeming love of God in Christ, even they have the uneasy feeling that the first pillar, the doctrine of the Fall, has been irretrievably undermined, and totters on its base, no longer capable of bearing its former share of the super-incumbent weight. There are, indeed, those who urge that it is now a source of weakness rather than of strength to the fabric which it supported for so long and should be razed to the ground."
> (*The Ideas of the Fall and of Original Sin*, London: Longman's, Green, 1929, pp. 8-10)

This brings me to my last observation, which I regard as substantial. *Divine Principle* seems to explain the predicament of man almost entirely by reference to the account in *Genesis* II and III, expounded independently of Christology. Both Catholic and Protestant theologians insist that the mysterious doctrine of original sin cannot be illuminated or seen in its correct setting unless the primary reference is to the New Testament revelation of the divine salvific will through the incarnation of God in Jesus Christ. True, much of the older systematic theology, especially in the Reformation tradition, has followed the same methodology as that of *Divine Principle* in this question. The protest of Karl Barth has made a profound impression in the present century:

> "The incline obviously begins at the point where we think we have to create the message of sin from some other source than that of the message of Jesus Christ. This forces us to ask for an independent normative concept, and to move forward to the construction of it, and we fall at once into the whole arbitrary process.... And why should we not avoid the mistake at the point where it begins? What reason is there for that first belief that the doctrine of sin must precede Christology and therefore be worked out independently of it? The belief is a traditional one which has seldom been questioned but has usually been treated as more or less self-evident. In opposition to it we maintain the simple thesis that only when we know Jesus Christ do we really know that man is the man of sin, and what sin is, and what it means for man.... Because the God against whom the man of sin contends has judged this man, and therefore myself as this man, in the self-offering and death of Jesus Christ His Own Son, putting him to death and destroying him; ... Because the verdict passed in His resurrection from the dead unmasks this old man, showing what everyman is before God, and therefore what I myself am before Him, the man who is judged and put to death and destroyed. All this came upon Jesus Christ for every one of us and therefore for me, in our place and therefore in my place.... Because He is the One who has done this for us, the verdict of God passed in His resurrection and revealed in His being and living and speaking and witness is relevant to all men and therefore to ourselves.... In this verdict we learn what God knows about us, and therefore how it really is with us.... The fact that man is a sinner, and what his sin is, is

something that in the last resort we can measure properly and fully only by that which on the New Testament understanding is man's salvation, the redemptive grace which comes from God to man."
(*Church Dogmatics*, Vol. IV, Part 1, E.T. Edinburgh: Clark, 1956, pp. 389-91.)

This insight of Karl Barth is shared by Christian theologians today, both Protestant and Catholic, who take seriously the theology of sin. They do not look first to *Genesis* II and III for the revelation of Christian hamartiology, but to I *Corinthians* and *Romans*. Karl Rahner sums it up from the viewpoint of Catholic theology: "The fact that the mystery of original sin has its ground in the mystery of the bestowal of sanctifying grace also explains why the actual doctrine of original sin only appears in Scripture when the divinization of man by the Pneuma of God is explicitly grasped.... Original sin and being redeemed are two existentials of the human situation in regard to salvation, which at all times determine human existence" (*Sacramentum Mundi*, Vol. 4, s.v. "Original Sin").

In this perspective, I submit, our present discussion of the Fall and sin of man can only be proleptic, pointing forward to and presupposing the doctrine of Redemption and Restoration.

Freedom and the Will: A Unification Theory

Herbert Richardson

In this paper I outline that understanding of the will and of freedom which I believe is implicit in *Divine Principle*. *Divine Principle* offers important suggestions for further thinking: the notion of polyspheric willing and the concept of freedom as perfect justice are two such ideas. They are important for theology, for ethics, and for politics. Unification thought rejects the individualistic model of human actions presupposed by the teleological/deontological debate. It also rejects the communal model of human action presupposed by contextualists and Marxists. In my judgment, it offers resources to help us think beyond the dilemmas faced by contemporary thinkers.

Willing as a Polyspheric Act

Unification theology describes human action as polyspheric. For example, Moon says we must act on the "individual, familial, tribal, national, world, and God levels." Again, the scope of salvation is said to apply to the religious, political, economic, educational, linguistic, scientific, familial, and individual spheres.

Unification theology does not have, as far as I know, any theoretical conception of the human act as polyspheric. However, in my judgment, such a conception is implicit in its various descriptions of action. My goal, in this paper, is to outline a theoretical conception of human freedom as polyspheric action. My goal is not to be original, but to attempt to unify several theories of action. In so doing, we will come to see that the polyspheric character of human action is already understood.

The word "sphere" is here defined as a level, or dimension, of action which has a unique end, or purpose. The unique ends, or purposes, of action are:

the economic, or "event-forming"
the scientific, or "rule-forming"
the social, or "group-forming"
the linguistic, or "meaning-forming"
the spiritual, or "character-forming"
the judicial, or "judgment-forming"

The distinctiveness of the spheres, or dimensions, pertains to the *uniqueness* of their several ends. Events, rules, groups, meaning, character and judgment are not only different ends, but they are incomparably different, i.e., unique. This is why they are not merely several ends that might belong to the same sphere, but are several ends each belonging to *different* spheres.

Ethical theories have considered these various spheres in relation to the conception of the rightness, or goodness, of action. For example, Kant discussed whether the rightness of an action was determined by whether it produced a good-yielding happiness, or whether it conformed to a rule capable of universalization. The Kantian perspective, challenged by later utilitarianism, and recently developed by the teleological/deontological debate, discriminates two distinct spheres of action: the rule-forming and the event-forming. Every act both produces an event and also expresses a rule. The rule it expresses relates *both* to the event-forming and the rule-forming spheres, namely, that (1) if I act in such a way, then the event I seek will happen, and (2) if I act in such a way, then the possibility of *acting* (as a way of producing events) will be maintained.

The rule-forming dimension of human action seeks to develop, or maintain, the order within which human action can be rationally purposive and, therefore, *free*. I call this dimension the "scientific" sphere. (It is traditionally called the "moral" sphere.)

The event-forming dimension of human action includes those things which can be intended as particular ends of human action for the sake of the happiness they bring.

Human actions can aim at causing an event which brings happiness *and* at expressing, or establishing, a rule which maintains the rationally purposing character of human action itself. In fact, any particular choice—or aspects of that choice—includes both these spheres. They are two dimensions of the same choice and not two different choices. This is why we speak of the polyspheric character of human action.

However, from this analysis, we can also see that a human action can include not merely event-forming and rule-forming dimensions, but also several others: the group-forming, the meaning-forming, and the character-forming.

The group-forming dimension of every act is of special interest to contextual ethics. Every action has a social character. It reaffirms a set of social relations, or it can expand or decrease that set of relations. Sexual intercourse can have an amative as well as procreative function, i.e., it can *bond* two persons thereby creating a *group*. For example, abortion is an act which, whether right or wrong, *excludes* prenatal life from the group of moral subjects. All human actions have some group-forming character. This group-forming character is always seen in manners, courtesy, and style.

In a society with high group consciousness, the *contextual* character of human action is the most important criterion of moral rightness and wrongness. How an action *affects* the group is the most important consideration in evaluating it. In Christianity, with its strong emphasis on God's desire to unify the human race, there is an ethical disposition towards universality, and this becomes a contextual value that affects our evaluation of all human actions. Human actions that establish social solidarity with a more universal community have a greater worth than those which have a particularistic tendency.

A fourth dimension of every human action is the linguistic. All human action is *significative*. Just as speech is a form of action, so action is a form of speech—especially moral speech. More simply, whenever we do something (for we do what we think is right), this shows what we mean by our words. In societies where action is systematically at variance with words, language itself is destroyed. That is, people learn that words do not mean what they say, but they mean what is done. Because all action is significative, therefore, all action forms language.

Recent studies of Nazi and Communist destruction of language through propaganda help us appreciate how all action has a linguistic dimension. Hence, a moral action must not only aim at a good, act according to a right-rule, and create a universal context, but it must also tell the truth. It must maintain the meaning of human life by expressing truth in action. If it fails to do this, it does injury to the linguistic sphere.

A fifth sphere of action is the spiritual. Here I define the spiritual as that which pertains to a person because he is formed by the effects of his own free action. While, on the one hand, our acts express our competence as free beings, one of their chief effects is also to shape our character. Every free action has a reflexive effect upon the subject of that action and, taken cumulatively, our actions determine our character and make us the kind of people we are.

Were our actions, in all their other spheres, morally laudable, we would tend to become (through their reflexive effects) persons possessing ideal moral character. As it is, however, the accumulated failures of our actions in their other spheres have an impact upon our own character. We become diverted from our "true selves," blind to moral truth, and now formed in the image of our own sin.

But the formation of character is not merely the reflexive consequence of actions that pertain to other spheres. Just as there are sphere-specific actions in the order of language (e.g., correcting grammar) or in the order of social relations (e.g., getting married), so there are sphere-specific actions in the order of character formation (e.g., the prayerful imitation of Christ, or confession or penance). Sphere-specific actions have, as their primary aim, the production of the personal character of the moral subject, strengthening his capacity to act rightly in the several other moral spheres. However, his right or wrong action in the several other moral spheres also reflexively affects his own character (in his ability to act rightly).

There remains one further sphere of human action. We have, to this point, discriminated five functions: the event-forming, the rule-forming, the group-forming, the meaning-forming and the character-forming. We have suggested that these functions define five dimensions, or spheres, that pertain to *every* human action:

the economic—event-forming
the scientific—rule-forming
the social—group-forming
the linguistic—meaning-forming
the spiritual—character-forming

I have also suggested that ethical theoreticians have given consideration to the qualities of these spheres as criteria for moral action. Hence, teleological, deontological, contextual, and meta-ethical theories relate to the first four spheres and traditional spirituality is specifically interested in the fifth.

The problem that now arises is how are these several spheres that exist *within each human act* to be reciprocally related and harmonized? Because they are quite distinct from one another, they often do exist in disharmony. For example, a person can choose a happiness-yielding event by violating a universal rule, or can follow the rule and not be happy. Or a person can affiliate with a universal community and be obliged to violate rules of significative moral language, or vice versa. The fact of the matter is that it is difficult to act in such a way that there is harmony among the several dimensional tendencies of our actions. We usually establish a unity within our actions by raising the moral criterion of one or another of the spheric tendencies to a principle of primacy. (For example, Kant extracts the principle of moral action from the rule-forming sphere.)

Because all of the spheres are *intrinsically* necessary to every action, one cannot argue that any one is more important than the others. Moreover, because the values they individually involve are incomparable, one cannot argue from a *hierarchical* ordering as a way of producing unity. For these reasons, the sole way to *unify* the spheric values in human action is by *harmonizing* them. This activity of harmonization must itself be yet *another unique sphere of action:* the *judicial.*

The moral activity which seeks to establish the best possible harmonization among the several moral tendencies within every action is justice. Justice is the weighing of incomparables which takes effect as a judgment giving specific form to the polyspheric act. In this act, a judgment is expressed as how best to include (or exclude) the various spheric tendencies.

Under conditions of sin, the best justice we can obtain involves the sacrifice of some values and some spheres in order to save others. Under these conditions, the harmony justice can obtain is, at best, a balancing of goods and evils, rights and wrongs, accommodations and hopes. The sole principle relating to such "imperfect justice" I wish specially to note, however, is that justice always aspires to full redemption. Hence, justice must always act so that the possibility of perfect future harmonization is maximally maintained.

Even under conditions of human perfection, i.e., perfect harmonization, the activity of justice is necessary. For example, just as in music any theme can be expressed in several variations which are all equally perfect (their difference does not arise from degrees of imperfection), so in even a perfect world there is need for justice. The judicial sphere, therefore, is essential to every human action. It is the judgment which establishes the maximal harmony of moral tendencies within the human act and, even in a perfect state, creates multiple new perfect harmonies.

Freedom as the Perfection of the Will

The concept of freedom pertains, in the normative case, to the act of *perfect willing*. A free will is a will which chooses as it should. Failures of a will to act as it should are lacks of its perfect freedom. Hence, a will which is unfree has lost its perfection—chief of which is losing its capacity to act justly, or to harmonize all the sphere-specific values which it simultaneously desires.

When I desire both that the moral rule for my act be universalizable and I also choose a good that I would not also want for everyone else, then my two desires are in contradiction. This contradiction in my own desires cannot be harmonized and, hence, I myself cause my own unfreedom or my own inability to will perfectly.

Of course, I could will freely if I could bring my desires into harmony. As Anselm noted, the truly free man wants only what is right and all that he wants is right: hence, there is harmony between his two specific desires.

Given the fallenness of man, the sole being whom we can imagine possessing perfect freedom is God. God's will is perfectly free because all that God desires is capable of harmonization. There is, therefore, no limitation on God's freedom or His creative power. In this conception, the moral perfection of God is the basis for His power and sovereignty. In the same way, when a human being overcomes sin (the self-contradiction in his own desires) he is capable of willing like God and gains in His capacity for creative (free) action.

The cause of all unfreedom is internal disharmony of desires. The supposition that there are external constraints on one's freedom confuses the fact that one cannot have everything one desires with the idea of a limitation of one's power of free choice. This limitation arises in the encounter with two types of situations: moral and non-moral. A moral limitation to one's willing is encountered when the will of another impedes one's own desires. Since, in this case, one can gain one's own desires only at the cost of denying the will of another, such a purpose would stand in contradiction with the sphere-values of rule universality and of group-extension (at least!). If one should go ahead and attain some particular desire by sacrificing these other values, then one would act in contradiction to those very conditions that maintain even relative free will. Hence, a moral impediment to one's choice cannot be construed as a limitation on one's freedom—even though it may be an impediment to one's willing.

The same type of argument applies also to being limited by non-moral entities. Obviously, in such situations, when someone cannot have what he desires, then he should transform his desire to what is really possible. To want what is not possible is to create one's own unfreedom. It is a *self*-limitation on one's freedom to desire what is impossible, a self-limitation that can only be removed by transforming one's desires so that they can be effectively willed. Hence, it is no limitation on freedom that a person wants what he cannot attain through his choice.

The imagination that external impediments to our actions constitute limitations on our freedom arises from regarding freedom as a form of *mere willing* (*velle*). Mere willing, sometimes called *spontaneous* willing, is the *abstract* idea of a single desire taken in separation from the conditions of *the moral act*. Where persons act spontaneously, giving momentary precedence to a single sphere-specific willing over the other willings that are also necessary, then their patterns of choices evidence a back-and-forth choice and reversal, doing and undoing, as if they could not make up their minds. But, marrying today, divorcing tomorrow, marrying again, divorcing again, or wanting children, complaining when one has them, impregnation, abortion—these are not the patterns of action of free beings. These patterns reveal an actor engaged in constant self-contradiction of his own previous actions. That such a person *feels* he acts spontaneously, abstracting the dominant desire of the moment from its place in the polyspheric moral self (and from the continuity of time) does not make his actions free. His spontaneous actions are not free because they never are effective; they are constantly being undone by the subject of these actions himself, who thereby destroys his own freedom.

The concept of human freedom, like the concept of God's freedom, pertains to the conditions of volitional *power* or *effective action*. Freedom is the perfection of willing, i.e., the condition of its efficacy. Without freedom, our actions always lack full efficacy. As Augustine said, a sinful act is *non posse non peccare*, a deficient (not an efficient) willing. In the same way, according to Augustine, a free act is one which is perfectly efficacious because it cannot fail to achieve its purposes.

For man, at least, the concept of efficacious willing (i.e., free will) must be determined with respect to the temporal order. (We shall later see this is also true for God.) Efficacious willing is willing through which a man is able to attain his ends, or shape his own life, through the whole course of time. This requires that he act in a pattern of choices which are not self-contradictory, but reciprocally harmonious and self-reinforcing. A sinful man, day by day, acts to undo his previous day's choices. A man possessing freedom acts, day by day, to build on (thereby reaffirming and also extending) what he has previously chosen. When this occurs, a man creates his future because his past actions are efficacious in making his future purposes become real.

The characteristic of free human willing is efficacy in shaping the future by creating continuity of events in time that bring a person eventually to attain his goals. A conception of human freedom is not adequate if it does not account for the capacity of a human being to direct the course of his life towards his own ultimate future and, through his own free acts, to shape his own destiny. Particularly the conception of "consumer freedom"—the lady in the supermarket confronted by multiplicities of possible choices (products) from which she spontaneously chooses what she prefers—is a false conception of freedom. In fact, this notion of "consumer freedom"—emphasizing spontaneous reaction to externally provided possibilities—is a notion betraying the idea of freedom itself. It is a 1984 conception of language where true freedom is taken away in the name of "freedom."

True freedom rests on the possibility of fulfilling one's purpose. Where this purpose is the goal of an entire life, true freedom requires *perseverance* as its chief virtue. In the temporal order, a long-range purpose can be attained only step by step, through a series of intermediate purposes which lead towards one's final goals. This means that human freedom requires the exercise of the full range of virtues essential to willing: for example, the exercise of reason in planning and scheduling tasks and the exercise of justice in balancing and harmonizing the various tasks. The characteristic of a free being is that, from the point of view of his purpose, the course of his life can be seen to have a rational order expressive of that purpose.

These same considerations also apply to God's purposes for His creation. If God has a purpose for creation—and He must have since He created the world—then that purpose must be exhibited as a rational order of God's action in time. The debate among theologians whether such a "philosophy of history" is possible only reveals how little they understand the character of freedom. For Reinhold Niebuhr, for example, the "freedom" of God is the same spontaneous arbitrariness of a housewife in a supermarket—a "freedom" unrelated to purposive action. Hence, quite consistent with his denial of God's true freedom and any philosophy of history, Niebuhr also denies that God has a purpose for *this* world.

If God *has* a purpose for this world, then the realization of that purpose must take the form of a rational order of historical laws and events that move towards its attainment. In the contemporary world, only Unification and various revolutionary theologies understand this principle and seek to exhibit it as a philosophy of history. These theologies understand the basic truth that if God is the free, purposing Lord of history, then history itself must exhibit a purposive order.

In time, freedom is manifested as an order of events which leads toward the attainment of a goal or goals. To this activity, planning and harmonizing are of crucial importance. However, it has already been pointed out that freedom is, first of all, a spiritual activity. It does not depend upon time. Rather *time* depends upon *it*. Freedom is a supra-temporal activity by which a person determines purposes and possibilities. The temporal act of a person merely expresses, in another order, what has already been established as a spiritual reality: the judgment which, in its perfect form, is the free act of the will.

Unification and Traditional Christology: An Unresolved Relationship

Durwood Foster

In the effort now gaining momentum[1] to understand and respond to the fresh theological energy of the Unification movement, Christological issues obviously have a pivotal role. *Divine Principle* states that the most important questions of all fall within this area.[2] This would necessarily be so in the broad sense of "Christ" standing for the axial event or person on which any religion is grounded, but it is particularly the case with respect to an intensely messianic movement such as Unificationism. Moreover, standing as it does on its own historic norm of Jesus as the Christ, the mainstream Christian tradition naturally focuses its assessment of any new religious movement in Christological terms, as we have seen in provisional pronouncements upon Unification belief by committees of the National Council of Churches and the Association of Theological Schools. Since Sun Myung Moon launched his mission expressly to unify world Christianity,[3] it is inevitable that the most sensitive flash points of discussion would arise within the interpretation of Christ.

In, through and under an immense variegation of terminology and conceptual detail, "Christ," in general, stands for the decisive means by which the purpose of the world is rectified and fulfilled. In historic Christianity as well as in Unification teaching, this decisive means is envisaged in two primary instantiations: (a) the coming of the Christ in First Century Palestine, and (b) his expected return to consummate history. While the dialectical relation between the two instantiations is at the heart of any living Christology, attention within our present space shall be addressed to the first, the Christ who has already come. This is not to deny that the most arresting claims of Unificationism arise with respect to the second, that is, the returning Christ.[4] Such claims, however, are couched in terms that fundamentally depend upon the Unification understanding of the Christ as the historical Jesus, particularly what he left undone. Hence any responsible effort to comprehend and critically evaluate Unification messianic themes must join discussion at the level of the biblical and classical Christological data, as we now undertake to do.

1. The Humanity of Christ

One of the most deep-seated principles of Unification theology generally is its clear and emphatic recognition that "the providence of restoration cannot be fulfilled by God's power alone, but...is to be fulfilled by man's joint action with God."[5] It should be underscored what a notably Christological principle this is. In spite of obscurations that have occurred in the classical theological tradition (*viz.* the virtual theoretical annulment at some points of a *real* human participation in the salvific process—as has been tellingly analyzed in our time by Process Theology), it is elemental to the very notion of Christ that the setting free and making whole of the world is a divine *and* human action. In its widest peripheries this action intends to engage all of us and perhaps all creatures whatever, but its inner core, its definitive paradigm, is the Christ per se. "Christ" *means*, in other words, God *incarnate*, God *enhistoricized*, God *enhumanized*, God *with us* (Immanuel). In its very essence it is a *theanthropic* notion, and the clearer it becomes the more firmly *both* its terms—the divine *and* the human—are articulated. On the foundational witness of the Gospels, such an articulation was achieved in the climactic orthodox formula of full humanity inseparably as well as unconfusedly united with full deity in Christ's person. It was lucidly upheld, to cite another shining example, by St. Anselm in his exposition of Christ's work, in which the question "Why God-man?" (*Cur Deus-homo?*) cannot be answered except by seeing the integral role of both deity and humanity in the creative and restorative process. In spite of the firm anchorage of this truth in the great landmarks of classical tradition, most scholars would accept D.M. Baillie's judgment[6] that it was a special service of the nineteenth century search for the original Jesus to bring an "end to Docetism" and thus vindicate radical humanity as Christologically axiomatic. Assessed along this line, Unification Christology gets high marks for its categorical affirmation of human soteriological responsibility in indefeasible give and take with God's. At the christic center of soteriology this means a theologically healthy predisposition in behalf of Christ's unimpeachable humanity.

2. The Deity of Christ

On the other side of the basic christic formula the situation is less clear, and yet there are in Unificationism propitious elements for a strong thematization also of Christ's deity. As a cardinal premise of such thematization, Unification commitment to a radical God-centeredness is unequivocal. In emphatic opposition to communism as well as the secularist "death of God" strain in recent theology, this continues to be a main plank in the Moonie platform.[7] Nor has there been, in general terms, any failure in Unificationism to apply God-centeredness to the salvific process. On the contrary, it has been insistently maintained that God is the world's Creator and Restorer in incommensurably greater degree than humanity, whose (indeed real!) "portion of responsibility" is itself grounded in divine will and nature. This determinative theistic note is conspicuous also in the existential religious witness of Moonies. Such a theistic frame of reference is surely pertinent in assessing the broad Christological intentionality of Unificationism, even if it does not *ipso facto* insure congruence with the orthodox model of Christ's person, at least not immediately or objectively.

At present, *Divine Principle* stops short of the full traditional affirmation of christic divinity as that was established at Nicaea, Constantinople, and Chalcedon.[8] A pivotal formulation of its view is that while Jesus "may well be called God," because he exemplified individual human perfection, "he can by no means be God himself."[9] This is typologically a "low" Christology of the Antiochean type, as opposed to the "high" one of Alexandrian tradition. In the former, Christ's humanity is substantive and his divinity adjectival; he is the divine man, that is to say, the perfectly God-related or God-indwelt man. In the Alexandrian tradition on the other hand, there is an obverse focus. The humanity is adjectival and the divinity substantive; Christ is the incarnate or enhumaned God. Chalcedon's achievement was to synthesize Antioch and Alexandria, not in logical explanation but nonetheless in faithful affirmation. Unificationism so far does not espouse this synthesis, even though both sides of the dialectic underlying it come to expression in *Divine Principle*. The latter can aver that it "does not deny the attitude of faith held by many Christians that Jesus is God, since it is true that a perfected man is one body with God."[10] This phraseology of the unity of "body" has per se much to recommend it, harmonizing not only with a prime image like Colossians 2:9[11] but also with the pervasive biblical feel for body—not to speak of its analogical suggestiveness in terms of modern physics and ontology. But though ostensibly saving the phenomenon of the New Testament witness to Christ (on this, its deific side) *Divine Principle*'s mode of predication seems unmistakably intended in the Antiochean sense of Paul of Samosata and dynamic monarchianism, rather than of Nicene and Chalcedonian orthodoxy. What clinches this is the express denial that Christ can be God himself (tantamount *prima facie* to negating the Nicene *homoousios*, the "very God of very God"). While it can be said that fulfilled humanity "attains" and "possesses" deity, "feeling exactly what God feels and knowing God's will,"[12] the Christological mode of union one must judge to be construed morally or functionally rather than ontologically. Christ, who is rightly seen to be fully human, while flawlessly united with divine purpose, does not really share divine nature as Chalcedon affirms in the idea of the hypostatic or personal union.

Do we confront here, then, a basic antithesis between Unificationism and classical Christian orthodoxy? Before jumping to this conclusion, a number of considerations invite attention.

One concerns the overall situation in contemporary theology. Beyond Christendom's multifarious long standing divisions and irrespective of ecumenical progress, it is a commonplace that since mid-century there has occurred a further bewildering break up of theological cohesion. Christology particularly is "up for grabs." Jesus Christ is more or less incontestably the norm of Christian faith, but there is sorely lacking consensus as to what the Christ norm means. The World Council of Churches itself operates under a banner ("Jesus Christ as God and Savior") which in the eyes of many theologians is dubiously orthodox, omitting as it does to register the categorical humanhood of Christ. Mindful of the recent ruckus over Küng and Schillebeeckx, our question here would be whether there remains enough conceptual unison in mainstream theology—outside, let us say, the Roman magisterium—to render a credible judgment as to the orthodoxy of the Unification construal of Christ's person. It does not settle this question simply to ascertain literal disparity between the classical creeds and Divine Principle. Only for fundamentalism would that be the case. Mainstream theologians have long recognized that a kind of historical parallax—a basic displacement in conceptual position— must be reckoned with in any attempt to state what Nicaea and Chalcedon mean for us today. This is the premise and hermeneutical task of all constructive work in theology and Christology.

One might ask in this whole connection whether Unificationism appears to be any less orthodox regarding Christ's divinity than, for example, such a notable mainstream theologian as Paul Tillich. There is probably no major constructive theologian of modern times at whom the charge of heresy has not been hurled, and certainly Tillich has been so indicted. Nevertheless his reputation is unassailable as one of the "greats" among this century's systematic expositors of historic Christian faith. It was, of course, crucial to the figure Tillich cut in theology that he always evinced a will to stand in the orthodox tradition, that is to say, in what he took to be its authentic depth— wherefrom he mounted sharp criticism against the pervasive distortions he saw in current would-be versions of the tradition. Does Unificationism similarly manifest a will to valid orthodoxy as the implicit reference of its reforming and unifying zeal? There is evidence in Divine Principle that this is so—not only generally in the appeal to biblical authority, but with Christological specificity, for example, in not wanting to deny (as cited just above) "the attitude of faith of many Christians that Jesus is God," i.e., the banner of the World Council of Churches. Comparing further, Tillich's theology is also patently Antiochean. Jesus is the Christ inasmuch as he is essential or true *humanity* under the conditions of existence.[13] For Tillich it is synonymous to speak also of Jesus' *God*-manhood since essential humanness *ipso facto* embodies a normative God-relationship; where ideal human being is posited so, relationally, is God too. Paul of Samosata could readily have agreed with this. It is likewise quite parallel to *Divine Principle*'s language about Jesus' or anyone's (though till now Jesus was in fact the sole case) perfect humanity being "one body" with God and thus in a manner of speaking God.

Now there are in Tillich's system complementary elements which in significant degree make up for what might otherwise be assessed—in the specific thematization just adduced—as a serious Christological shortage.[14] These further elements, like additional particles in another ring of the atom, can be and are seen by many as, so to speak, balancing out the valence of Tillich's orthodox Christian identity. Pivotal in this regard are his trinitarianism, his profound doctrine of sin, and on the basis of these his incarnational thrust.[15] Essential God-humanhood, or the potentiality of ideal human life (which into itself as a kind of crowning matrix subsumes all finite potentiality), is equivalent to the Logos or second trinitarian *persona*. This essentiality or potentiality or Logos becomes incarnate when undistortedly instantiated as an existing human being—an event which, given the measure of the human plight, can only be a miracle of grace. Tillich never resolves the conceptual problems implicit here of so-called subordinationism in the Trinity and of differentiating the divine and human in Christ. But who would claim that anywhere in the tradition these problems have been altogether resolved? The point is simply that the affirmative role played in his thought by such elements greatly helps (in spite of his fairly numerous detractors) to credential Tillich as a mainstream theologian. They show in him a right minded *fides implicita* even though this may lack adequate Christological explicitation. Would it be too much to claim that a similar situation obtains with respect to most, if not all, individual theologians? Are they not as individuals, if not one-sidedly Antiochean in Christology, then (like Karl Barth) one-sidedly Alexandrian, wherewith their larger orthodoxy, if such can indeed be imputed, is then made out by their attitudinal orientation and such further complementary elements as we have alluded to?

If in any case we now ask whether there are corresponding complementary elements in Unification teaching, the answer is that there are but these so far are not fully developed in terms especially of their Christological implications. Noteworthy are (a) the intuition of the *gravity* of the human problem—a very important source, let it be recalled, in Anselm's derivation of the need for the God-man, (b) the envisagement of a *superhuman* power opposing restoration—a large factor in the so-called "classical" (Aulen) view of Christ's work and *its* correlative Christology, and (c) an affinity for the biblical theme of divine providence in history—which, while congenial to narrational process modes of thought, tends to weight Christological reflection against simplistic kinds of Ebionism and Adoptionism and toward a stress on divine involvement.

Divine Principle also has a brief section on the Trinity in which the notion of Logos is adduced and we are told, in a way intriguingly suggestive of Schleiermacher, that "Jesus and the Holy Spirit become one body centered on God."[16] This points promisingly in the direction of a doctrine of what is called the "economic" Trinity (the Trinity as historically and salvifically effectuated), but regarding the so-called "immanent" or internal Trinity there is a problem. To use Tillich again as a contrasting example, *his* fundamental ontology—aligned with Hegel and Western tradition—finds immanent trinitarianism spontaneously congenial; the inmost dialectic of God's life (the dynamic of being-itself) is triadic. Hence there is a convenient mutuality in Tillich of economic and immanent Trinity; the two symbolic constellations seem at least *prima facie* to be mutually supportive. But *Divine Principle's* fundamental ontology initially is arranged in such terms as the "fourfold position" and the "dual essentialities." Crassly put, we are primordially confronted with 4 and 2, rather than with 3. There is so far lacking, so far as I am aware, a thorough systematic mediation between these prime concepts (owing much, as they do, to such Chinese conceptual roots as the *yin-yang* motif) and classical Western trinitarianism. Such mediation is certainly not impossible; indeed, the present time is a *kairos* in which it particularly beckons. As it proceeds there figures to be a generative enrichment in Christological conceptuality—Unificationist and otherwise.

This occasions the further observation that Unification Christology is obviously still (*religionsgeschichtlich*) very young and inchoate, or to emphasize the positive, it is just now undergoing vigorous evolution. It is not inconceivable that the express negation of Christ's deity might be annulled; for it could be argued already on Unificationist grounds that this element, which flies in the face of Nicæa and Chalcedon, is gratuitous. Rev. Moon is still speaking, and one hears there is much esoterica which outside interpreters (like myself) have not seen. Moreover, a corps of able younger theologians are devotedly at work parsing and reconceptualizing the emerging parameters of Unification Christology. They are doing this in intense give and take with biblical, classical, and current models. It is not predictable, really, what may become of the trinitarian and other rudiments—the Logos motif, the accent of providence, the doctrine of deranged human nature and of Satan as superhuman evil to be overcome—which potentially conspire to generate a strong Christology on the divine as well as the human side. The Unification doctrine of Christ's person, from where it is now, *can* either diverge more widely from the Christian mainstream or move into clearer synthesis with it.

Which way Unificationism moves will be greatly influenced by the interplay of its own fundamental theological attitude of faith-disposition with those it encounters in the Christian mainstream. If the original Unification thrust, as most definitively given so far in *Divine Principle*, congeals into an anti-Nicene and anti-Chalcedonian slant, then the gap with the mainstream will widen. But if the classical heritage is appropriated in the spirit of positive demythologization or reinterpretation—the stance, for example, of Tillich, but also of all

creative mediating theologians—then Unificationists will find themselves, at least at many points, collaborating in the common enterprise
of contemporary ecumenical theology. Standing with the classical
Christian tradition is, prior to one's specific conceptual lineaments, a
choice of existential orientation. At present it seems, in view of the
energetic program of advance study and dialogue being undertaken
from within Unification theology, that there exists in the latter a
potent disposition toward alliance and resynthesis with the Christian
heritage. Also crucial, however, will be the response(s) coming from
the other side—from the mainstream tradition. If it is a response
dominated by aloofness and defensive rejection, this will exacerbate
antithesis and tend to objectify Unification Christology into heresy by
defining it as such. If on the other hand, the would-be heirs of biblical
and classical Christian faith respond with humility and openness, glad
for any opportunity to witness to Christ, seeking with whoever will
the truth in love, they may—while hopefully enlarging their own
vision—significantly facilitate a kind of reconversion of Unification
Christology into resonance with the ecumenical mainstream.

3. The Work of Christ and its Incompletion

Yet we may be thinking too fractionally when we envisage an
orthodoxizing of Unification Christology without having fully pondered
the wider soteriological setting. According to the well known maxim
of Melanchthon, "to know Christ is to know his benefits"; the
doctrine of Christ's person cannot be seperated from the understanding of his work. However well otherwise disposed to christic
orthodoxy, Unificationism could still be unable to harmonize with
mainstream Christology what has generally been taken as *Divine
Principle*'s view of the failure of Jesus. For the classical thematization of
Christ developed as a conceptual doxology to Jesus and his achievement. It was not intended as a hypothetical formula stating what must
be conjoint divine-human pivot of salvific process, which might then
be applied to the Christ yet to come. Classical Christology emerged
rather as a functional ensemble of religious language saying something
ultimate about a particular man's life, death, and resurrection. Its

communicative intelligibility was and is the same as its faith-validity, namely, its witness that God with Jesus has accomplished our salvation. When something substantively corresponding to that is experienced and believed, classical Christology—demythologized and reinterpreted but still itself—remains viable and necessary. On the other hand, when the experience of Jesus as Savior is lacking or severely diminished, the intentionality of Nicaea and Chalcedon becomes otiose and false.

Of course these generalizations cannot offhand yield definite results in our present discussion, because they require qualification in two directions. In one, the fact must be weighed that biblical-Christian tradition does not say *simply and only* that the Christ as Jesus has already accomplished salvation. In spite of the theological position known as "realized eschatology," the clear thrust of the tradition is that some part of the salvific process remains unfulfilled, so that Christ must return to consummate his work. In the other direction, Unificationism does not say *simply and only* that Jesus failed. On the contrary, there are salient respects in which *Divine Principle* affirms his achievement. Thus we have in the abstract a possible congruence between the two sets of variables: orthodoxy holds Jesus (a) did succeed, and yet (b) not entirely; Unificationism holds he (x) did not entirely, and yet (y) did succeed. The sums of the pairs of variables are in some way "y." They both add up to what is respectively construed as the full salvation of the world. But how decisive is the proportional difference between the anterior and posterior terms—between the first and the second instantiations of Christ?

Unificationism teaches that Jesus was divinely sent (a motif counting toward his deity) to bring about the restoration and fulfillment of creation. Now the aim of creation according to *Divine Principle* embraces the distinct levels of (i) individual perfection, (ii) founding a God-centered family, and (iii) actualizing world dominion, i.e., establishing the Kingdom of Heaven on earth.[17] Jesus, while attaining the first of these and thus entitled, as noted above, to be regarded as "one body with God," was prevented from accomplishing the latter two. He did not marry and procreate, nor did he establish God's realm throughout the earth. Thus, in a nutshell, it might appear that two-thirds of the messianic task is still outstanding, waiting to be completed by the second christic instantiation.

   This arithmetic would be misleading, however, for Unificationism holds that when frustrated in his primary mission Jesus picked up, as it were, an alternative mission also provided by divine providence— that of dying for the sins of the world. "We can never deny," says *Divine Principle*, "the magnitude of redemption by the cross."[18] It seems in fact that the indemnity rendered by Christ's death, though mainly represented as a back-up plan on God's part, was quite necessary to the salvific process. We are told that "Jesus, who came as the second Adam...had to serve and honor God from the position of being abandoned by him, in order to be able to restore mankind from the bosom of Satan to that of God" and that "herein lies the complex reason that God had to forsake Jesus when he was crucified."[19] Since *Divine Principle* elsewhere claims novel revelatory insight that Jesus did *not* come into the world to die—a matter on which it thinks all Christians till now were mistaken,[20] there is a strain upon coherency at this point. But this not unusual situation in Christology does show in any event, more of an ambivalence than might first meet the eye in the Unification thematization of Christ's work. Insofar as the passage just quoted is given weight—and there is a more than negligible line of thought supporting it in *Divine Principle*—how can it be said that Jesus failed?

   One might therefore speak of the tradition as, indeed, like *Divine Principle*, recognizing with respect to Jesus *two* wills and providences of God, one subtending the plenary establishment of the kingdom and the other entailing sacrificial self-offering as exacted by the obduracy of evil which provisionally thwarts the first providence. The first might be said to be willed by God primordially but nonetheless contingently, since there is the component of human response. The second we could say to be willed consequently, in view of the fact of human sin and guilt that actually arises.[24] Historically this would be the infra-lapsarian position, to which the Unification view is clearly akin. However, instead of construing the phases of divine will in temporal sequence, theological tradition has in the main integrated them logically as a complex providential unity, in effect opting for a kind of dialectical supra-lapsarianism. This avoids a bifurcation of divine intentionality, which Christian consciousness has increasingly tended to find abhorrent. In the last analysis, both infra- and supra-lapsarianism express something essential in the Christian self-consciousness, as both are likewise transcended by the aporias of eternity and time and grace and freedom. Here, as at other points, what might appear to be an impasse between Unificationism and tradition can also be seen as an unresolved struggle within both.

But if *Divine Principle* is not as novel as it assumes on Jesus' destiny of the cross, it does diverge sharply from tradition in assigning major responsibility for Jesus' failure to John the Baptist. "Since the time of Jesus till the present," we are told, "no one has been able to reveal this heavenly secret."[25] What now makes the insight possible is said to be an abandonment of the fear "to remove old traditional concepts," enabling a more accurate reconstruction from the biblical data, which is corroborated by occult communication.[26] Yet, whatever hermeneutics might make of the methodology, it is not out of line with modern research into the Baptist to conclude that there was, far more than the received stereotype would suggest, a complex tension between his movement and that of Jesus. In a broad sense, therefore, *Divine Principle* can hardly be gainsaid in theorizing that John failed to prepare the way of Christ in the measure that he might have. Not only is this historically plausible, it also accords with the theological insight that the "Christ event" is perforce more inclusive than Jesus in isolation.[27] Thus what constituted the event as itself, what caused it to succeed so far as it did succeed or fail if it did fail, was undoubtedly in appreciable degree John the Baptist. We can recognize here once more a healthy tendency in *Divine Principle* to envisage in the salvific process a genuine human contingency, one rightly seen to be inevitably social even at its nucleus. The work of Christ, concentrated decisively in Jesus, nevertheless involves in preparation, execution, and extension—and certainly in fruition and frustration—what perhaps finally is the whole company of history. Patently, as types of the rest of us, it engages those *dramatis personæ* who are center stage with the main protagonist.

Now if something like this is consistent with *Divine Principle's* insight into the role of the Baptist, it is only fair to ask if it is not likewise the witness of the classical Christian mainstream. Does not the latter also say that the flawless input to God's realm of Jesus' own will and effort was and still is conditioned positively and negatively by all the viscissitudes and characters of the human drama? The work of Christ thus is complete (= perfect) in Jesus and incomplete wherever else we look. But if so the question would be: why pick out the Baptist so egregiously? What about Judas, or Mary, or Peter, or oneself? A valid insight can be forfeited if overdrawn. This is not to deny that *Divine Principle*, with its frequent flashes of historical intuition, can make us more sharply aware of a lack of coordination between John and Jesus. But the fundamental principle of the human "portion of responsibility," anchored in the Christ's own real humanity and distributed through the whole web of his interpersonal relations, would be obfuscated by individuated scapegoating. The tradition itself incurs this danger in its stereotype of Judas. To the Baptist, without precluding the ambiguity research divulges, it still attributed the predominant image of witness. Would it be too much to suggest that, with a kind of synthetic or integral—as opposed to the more differential calculus—of *Divine Principle*, the classical witness shows here again a tendency to take up provisional failure into paradoxical victory—a dialectic historically concretized in the key moments of Cross and Resurrection? John, for all the blemishes of his own martyrdom, addresses the summed-up human question to Jesus (Matt. 11:3) and becomes a saint—a specially honored cooperator in the complete and incomplete work of Christ.

4. The Resurrection of Christ

From even so cursory a treatment of our subject as here undertaken we can hardly disengage without touching finally upon the Resurrection in its own right. Methodologically this is awkward, since we set out under the limitation of addressing the first as distinguished from the second instantiation of Christ. But the distinction between these instantiations—in spite of its plausibility and necessity—is in the Christian mainstream bridged and modified, if not blurred and annulled, precisely by the Resurrection. Besides, if in general theological forum Christology is, as we said, "up for grabs," this is *a fortiori* true of the conceptualizing of the Resurrection. Nevertheless, in looking back to the first epiphany of Christ, we seem at least *prima facie* to confront in the theme of Jesus' rising from the grave perhaps the most blatant of all the differences between Unificationist and mainstream interpretation. For it is a commonplace of modern scholarship that, however the event of Resurrection may or may not be understood, it—or at least belief in it—was absolutely crucial to the birth of Christianity. But Unificationism, on the other hand, though it does envisage his spirit in paradise, appears not to predicate resurrection of Jesus at all.[28]

In the tradition the Resurrection of Jesus means (i) that his kingdom-inaugurating mission, mediated now through the Holy Spirit or Living Christ, continues in spite of and in fact by virtue of the Cross, looking ahead to his return at the end of the present evil age; (ii) that the person of Jesus is validated (raised to God's right hand) as enduring norm of the christic and salvific process; and (iii) that there is in what God does with the Cross a triumph over the negativity of sin and death. Let us compare these points sequentially with Unification teaching.

Obviously nothing is more basic to Unificationism than the teaching that Jesus' failure to found the kingdom in the First Century does *not* amount to permanent defeat for God. The mission continues, structured now by a rather elaborate scheme of providential episodes (which give meaning to intervening history), but expedited by the Holy Spirit and the Living Christ.[29] At the end of the present age the second christic instantiation will establish the kingdom on earth. How, then, does this differ from the mainstream view? One idea put forward by Divine Principle is that the intervening work, between the first and second epiphanies of Christ, is spiritual only; wherefore physical renewal must await the procreative input of the Lord (and Lady) of the Second Advent. Yet it is also acknowledged, as Christian tradition would certainly maintain, that "spiritual changes...sanctify the human body...transforming it...to the temple where God may dwell."[30] And it also appears that the incorporation of persons into the unified family of the Second Advent is not construed in any literally genetic way, but rather volitionally and spiritually—though this certainly has its communal, institutional, and material aspects. But how then, in principle, does this differ from the mainstream?

Perhaps what we listed as the Resurrection's second traditional meaning is the crucial sticking point. Mainstream Christianity unequivocally posits Jesus as the enduringly normative Christ, whereas Unificationism appears to teach that the Lord of the Second Advent, while filling the same christic office, will be a separate and distinct human individual. Yet here too the seeming antithesis invites careful mediation. On the side of the mainstream, it could hardly be claimed that in theology today there is any conceptual unanimity at all as to how the subjective individuality of Jesus perdures in unison with the christic process. Indeed, there is no one way this was ever settled in tradition either, although a broad consensus has existed and does— within Catholicism, the World Council, Orthodoxy, and the Evangelical groups—that the *character* of Jesus, his personal attributes of sacrificial humility, of righteous and forgiving love, are indefeasibly the marks of Christ. On the side of Unificationism, however, it would not seem to be denied that this is the case, whereupon the question would become whether the putative Lord of the Second Advent does in fact manifest the character in question. A categorical continuity, in any event, is posited between Jesus in the heavenly sphere and the one appointed as the new messiah in that Jesus reportedly calls and commissions and continues to communicate with him. Is this not in fact a symbolic way of expressing his identity or unison with Jesus? Moreover, in Divine Principle's notion of spirit persons being resurrected in those presently living on earth,[31] there is a suggestive analogy for the matter in hand. the Lord of the Second Advent could be construed as the Resurrection of Jesus, the delayed *parousia*, of which the New Testament appearances of the Risen One would then be the prolepsis. Divine Principle does not propose this, partly no doubt because of a different initial tack taken in the elucidation of resurrection which makes it awkwardly inappropriate for Jesus.[32] It would be a fairly superficial matter to revise the preclusive definition of resurrection (which in any case wants systematization with other connections within *Divine Principle*). But a deeper intuition may be at stake. The Unification movement *may* at bottom not be able to understand and constitute itself in terms of continuing lordship (supreme normativeness) of *Jesus* Christ. It *may*—in answer to the Baptist's question in Matthew 11:3—finally turn out to be looking for another. As we suggested in discussing the classical creeds and the work of Christ, that and only that would decide the issue. There are those who say Unificationism is a Christian heresy, just as it says in effect that Christendom will become heresy if it rejects the returning Christ. Heresy (from *heredein*) means firmly making up the mind. But is this firm deciding already done? Or are we right now still openly on the way to it? Obviously this essay believes there are significant senses, at least, in which the latter is the situation.

The third point of comparison promised above would concern the Resurrection as overcoming the negativity that is epitomized in the Cross: that is, the sway of sin and death—of injustice, meaninglessness, unlove, the destruction of persons. *Both* Unificationism and the Christian mainstream affirm this as God's aim and promise, for which the creation still groans and travails (Romans 8:22). Both see it as implemented by the indemnity of Jesus' Cross and the coming of the Spirit, though tradition couples the Spirit with an already witnessed Resurrection while this term is reserved by Unificationism for what will come. The issue is: how able to cope with sin and death is the Christ we know, the Christ of our own most personal witness? And the other side of this is Bonhoeffer's question: who is Christ for us today? Patently we have here a common ball park, even if we stand on relatively different sides. It would patently be as heretical to deny Christ's return as to deny his first epiphany and enduring lordship. Hopefully the dialogical interaction about this can proceed with a fairness, openness and mutual love that the risen and returning Christ, as in Matthew 25, would recognize and own.

FOOTNOTES

[1]One has in mind the wide-ranging dialogue being engendered by the Unification Theological Seminary and the Unification Church. The theological initiative of this open-ended program is remarkable. Still in its initial formative phases, Unification theology deliberately seeks to conceptualize and recognize itself in critical give and take with the entire contemporary theological and philosophical spectrum. For representative example of this burgeoning dialogue see Richard Quebedeaux and Rodney Sawatsky, eds., *Evangelical-Unification Dialogue* (Barrytown, New York: Unification Theological Seminary, Distributed by Rose of Sharon Press, Inc., 1979) and M. Darrol Bryant and A. Durwood Foster, eds., *Hermeneutics and Unification Theology* (Barrytown, N.Y.: Unification Theological Seminary, Distributed by the Rose of Sharon Press, Inc., 1980).

[2]*Divine Principle*, 5th ed. (Washington: Holy Spirit Association for the Unification of World Christianity, 1977), p. 205.

[3]Reverend Moon's organization emerged as the Holy Spirit Association for the Unification of World Christianity. As time has gone by, without relinquishing the aim thus posited, the intentionality of the term "unification" has seemed to become increasingly universal, embracing all religions as well as the sphere of the secular.

[4]I have dealt preliminarily with interpretive problems involved in these claims in a forthcoming article, "Christology and Hermeneutics, especially regarding Dialogue with Unification Theology," in Frank Flinn, ed., *Hermeneutics & Horizons: The Shape of the Future* (Barrytown, N.Y.: Unification Theological Seminary, Distributed by Rose of Sharon Press, Inc. 1981).

[5]*Divine Principle*, p. 283.

[6]D.M. Baillie, *God Was in Christ* (Scribner's, 1951), esp. Ch. II.

[7]Ignoring this point, many liberals have read Unification anticommunism simply as socio-economic conservatism. The conclusion seems precipitous, though it is true that the movement has yet to elaborate an economics and theory of society.

[8]Young Oon Kim, in her engrossing give and take with modern theology, *Unification Theology and Christian Thought* (New York: Golden Gate, 1975), p. 142, states that "In an age of theological reconstruction...like our own, Nicæa and Chalcedon look like moss-covered gravestones over a very dead past." Though its view of Christ's person is also sub-Nicene, such a decided negative tone toward classical Christology does not characterize *Divine Principle*. The less renunciatory mood of the latter, which is quasi-canonical as no other Unification statement is, may encourage the rising generation of Moonie theologians to approach the Christological tradition with a more conciliatory attitude than that evinced in Dr. Kim's book. Cf. Jonathan Wells, "Unification Hermeneutics and Christology," and Anthony Guerra, "The Historical Jesus and *Divine Principle*," in Flinn.

[9]*Divine Principle*, pp. 210-11

[10]*Divine Principle*, p. 209

[11]"For in him the whole fullness of deity dwells bodily" (RSV).

[12]*Divine Principle*, pp. 43, 140-41

[13]Paul Tillich, *Systematic Theology*, (University of Chicago Press, 1957), III, esp. pp. 138ff; for further on Tillich, see below.

[14]To be sure, some critics of Tillich have, like George Tavard in his *Paul Tillich and the Christian Message* (New York: Scribner's, 1962), not been willing to accept the proposed compensation. Tavard regards Tillich's literal disparity with Chalcedon as a fatal flaw in his would-be orthodoxy.

[15]Perhaps even more decisive is Tillich's clear assertion of the permanent normative bonding through the Resurrection of Jesus as the Christ with the salvific process, the "power of the new being" in Tillichian parlance. I have called attention to this point *vis-a-vis* Unification theology in my essay in Flinn.

[16]Flinn, p. 217

[17]*Divine Principle*, pp. 42-46, *passim.*

[18]*Divine Principle*, p. 142.

[19]*Divine Principle*, p. 226.

[20]*Divine Principle*, p. 152. A detailed theological analysis of *Divine Principle*'s coherence has to my knowledge not been undertaken.

[21]Albert Schweitzer, *The Quest of the Historical Jesus* (London: Black, 1910), *passim. Divine Principle* agrees that the first strategy foundered on the failure (which it blames on John the Baptist) to find requisite faith in Israel, but it does not follow Schweitzer in attributing to Jesus the thought of then *compelling* the Kingdom through his death.

[22]A fine example is William Temple, *Nature, Man and God* (London: Macmillan, 1935). Also deserving mention is the chess game analogy which goes back at least to William James. God, the master player, continuously shifts strategy to overcome the wiles of those who would thwart the divine goal of salvation.

[23]Yet *Divine Principle*'s tendency to *prescribe* marriage as humanly essential—by stipulating Adam and Eve rather than Jesus as the original human norm—is a latent problem in this regard. It tends in spite of everything to undermine the image of Jesus as perfect humanity. Contrastingly, the tradition recognizes and blesses marriage and parenthood as communally integral to human history while not required for the ideal fulfillment of the individual per se.

[24]Among recent writers Leslie Weatherhead has proposed distinctions with respect to divine will that broadly correspond with these. Cf. *The Will of God* (New York: Abingdon, 1944).

[25]*Divine Principle*, p.163

[26]*Divine Principle*, p. 163.

[27] John Knox was particularly effective in making this point. Cf., for example, *On the Meaning of Christ* (New York: Scribner's, 1947).

[28] *Divine Principle*, Ch. V, *passim*. In view of requirements of the modern intellect (p. 165), which knows the human body is not designed to live forever (p. 168), *Divine Principle* offers an elucidation of resurrection which in itself is a rather engaging piece of demythologization but which awkwardly results in a determination of the concept (as restoral from sin) which could not apply to Jesus, whose soul or spirit forfeits its body to Satan and goes to Paradise. To be sure, issues of coherency arise in respect to other passages in *Divine Principle*. For example, pp. 358-9 speak of Christians "setting up the resurrected Jesus as their object of faith," and of the "40-day resurrection period." Moreover, the view of Jesus' body as captured by Satan (p. 148), which prevents the achievement of the physical kingdom, seems to betray a latent need for the classical meaning of resurrection. Then too it is admitted (p. 172) that restoral of the spirit to God does after all entail spiritual changes, and that thus "in that sense it may be said that the physical body is also resurrected." Additionally there is the intriguing theme of the resurrection of those who have gone to the spirit world as they descend upon and assist, in the last days (primarily), enfleshed persons of the contemporary earth. This will occur in, through and around the messianic return. *Divine Principle* seems close here to seeing the Lord of the Second Advent as, not just the reactivator of the christic office, but the Resurrection of Jesus. Cf. below.

[29] *Divine Principle*, p. 216f., and Part II, *passim*.

[30] *Divine Principle*, p. 172.

[31] *Divine Principle*, pp. 187-91

[32] See footnote [28], above.

OTHER BOOKS ON THE UNIFICATION MOVEMENT

Distributed by
The Rose of Sharon Press, Inc.
G.P.O. Box 2432
New York, N.Y. 10116